The Wind Blows,
The Ice Breaks

The Wind Blows,
The Ice Breaks

Poems of Loss and Renewal
by Minnesota Poets

edited by
Ted Bowman
and
Elizabeth Bourque Johnson

NODIN PRESS

Many people have contributed to the enrichment of this volume. Our spouses and families, particularly, have lived with us and these pages for months. We affirm their on-going support and patience. We appreciate their contributions, cooperation and support.

Two persons deserve special mention. Jim Cihlar, poet and editor, read our manuscript and offered comments that enhanced this collection and the way in which it flows. Doug Lew, a Minnesota artist whose paintings are commissioned and exhibited nationally and abroad, created the cover painting for the book. He may be contacted at: www.douglew.com

ISBN 978-1-935666-00-4
Cover art: Doug Lew
Design and layout: John Toren

THIRD PRINTING, 2013

Library of Congress Cataloging-in-Publication Data
The wind blows, the ice breaks : poems of loss and renewal by Minnesota poets / edited by Ted Bowman and Elizabeth Bourque Johnson.
p. cm.
ISBN 978-1-935666-00-4
1. Grief--Poetry. 2. Loss (Psychology)--Poetry. 3. American poetry--Minnesota. I. Bowman, Ted. II. Johnson, Elizabeth Bourque.
PS571.M6W56 2010
811'.540809776--dc22

2010007372

Nodin Press, LLC
530 North Third Street
Suite 120
Minneapolis, MN
55401

Contents

The ice cracks beneath us . . .

The ice breaks, the wind blows ...

The sky begins to blue . . .

... and a bird sings.

Our Stories

ELIZABETH:

Grief was a black hole I fell into.

Coming home from the grocery store, I picked up the ringing phone to hear, "There's been an accident, ma'am." The room froze. The sheriff of Marshall County was calling from Plymouth, Indiana.

I don't know anyone in Indiana. Then I remembered that it was Martin Luther King, Jr., weekend, and my daughter Kristin, a freshman at Miami University of Ohio, was planning to spend the weekend with some Edina classmates at college in South Bend. *Indiana.*

Christmas break had been wonderful. Kris put ribbons in Julie's hair, gave fashion advice to Tricia, and went behind closed doors as always with Stephanie, the closest in age. Those two had been buddies from their earliest days, and Stephanie had missed Kris, her mentor and confidante, at least as much as her father and I had.

More phone calls. A night flight to South Bend. The bedside vigil and the cold reality of morning: Kristin was dead. Just 18, my first-born child was a "weather-related fatality" on an icy road in Indiana.

To try to explain grief or describe it can leave us staring open-mouthed, wondering what language can possibly express its shock, its grinding ache, and the total dislocation of one's life. Grief feels like madness. Life is out of control; you hardly recognize your own voice. One person talks incessantly, telling the story over and over as if to convince herself that the nightmare is real. Another person is mute.

Between these two poles there is a language that both expresses and processes the overwhelming experience of grief: the language of poetry. Poetry gathers in the huge, the unimaginable, the unbearable, that which threatens to smother us, and funnels it down into a few words—an image, a sound, a metaphor, a symbol—words that tell the truth and begin to make its reality possible to bear.

Friends gave me books of many kinds, including poetry, but most of those portrayed rainbows and sunsets, as if those beautiful sights had anything to do with the unfathomable darkness I was plummeting through. They seemed to brush away my real pain and rush me toward being all better. I needed something that told the truth about grief, how much it hurt and how hopeless it felt, and I needed words that got right to the point.

I needed poetry.

Years later I encountered poems that could have helped me, poems whose language and imagery reflected my feelings accurately and could have let me know that although I truly felt that I was going mad, I was doing the sanest, hardest work of my life and that I would eventually find my way out.

This book is an offering to persons in grief—whether from death, divorce, disease, or other losses—and to the people around them who want to understand and help. It is the book I wish my counselors and loving friends could have given me. I know that I'll encounter loss and grief again; this is the book I will need when that happens.

From the amazing riches of Minnesota poetry, Ted and I have selected poems that gather in the experience of many kinds of losses, not just death, and express it in honest, powerful ways. There are sad poems and angry poems, dark poems and hopeful poems. There are poems that just sit there with you when you are just sitting still. Because the path through grief is unique to each individual, the poems from each pen are unique, too.

The poems follow an arc from the first awareness of a loss through shock, anger, horror, and devastation and into the quiet time, the time of reorganization and renewal. Although mindful of the path-breaking work of Elisabeth Kubler-Ross, we have not attempted to define stages that follow each other in an orderly progression. Grief isn't like that; it circles through feelings in often unpredictable ways.

When I had worn out most of my friends (I was the constant talker), I wrote pages and pages in spiral notebooks, blurting out all that I felt. Once in a while I would stumble on a metaphor or image and write cleanly about it, and then I would find rest. The title of this book comes from one of those moments: I was walking on the ice in a frozen cove of Lake Superior one March day. The next morning the ice had broken up into huge chunks that were tossing in the waves—right where I'd been walking! That I had been in danger, that I could have drowned, that there was no warning, that I had no control, that the world is random—all those realizations were too much for me that morning. I started writing about the ice, and in those lines I took my first tiny step toward putting my loss into perspective: The world is dangerous; I am alive. Fierce winds blow us down, the ice cracks beneath our feet, yet somehow we go on.

Believe it or not, grief resolves, though once it seemed impossible. Birds sing, the sun comes out, we chuckle. Breathing is easier. You will hear the sounds of renewal in this collection.

Grief is a journey, but we don't have to travel alone. There's the story of the person who falls into a deep hole and can't get out, who calls for help to passers-by. A doctor writes a prescription and tosses it into the hole; a priest comes by and prays for awhile. Then a friend comes by and jumps into the hole.

"Why did you do that!" the person cries. "Now we're both stuck here."

"Not so," says the friend. "I've been here before, and I know the way out."

If you have a friend in the hole, jump in with this book in your hand. If you are the one in the hole, this book can help show you the way out.

TED:

For more than thirty years I have listened to people's stories about disruptive changes in their lives. Such events, I discovered, can shatter dreams, change lives and alter the future stories of individuals, families and communities. Simultaneously, I was reading poetry, memoir and fiction about change and loss. I came to the conclusion that each of these experiences was part of a similar process of giving voice. I began to link the two. Grieving people often found comfort, insight, provocation, or hope in the act of writing or reading peoms, or when responding to a poem or story I brought to share with them. My worlds of work, my own practice of writing, and the reading I was doing for pleasure and nurture merged.

The specific catalyst for this volume symbolizes that connection. A few years ago I found a slim volume of elegies and laments by Scottish poets in the Scottish Poetry Library in Edinburgh. The collection spoke to me, a visitor in that poetry-rich country. As I continued reading it, the thought occurred to me that a similar volume by Minnesota poets could be a resource for many. I remember thinking that grief is universal; it is neither Scottish nor Minnesotan.

There is an old adage that if something is unmentionable, it is also unmanageable. Words are necessary to move our feelings, thoughts and body messages from inside to outside. Poems can aid people in giving voice to their losses. For as we read someone else's words, we often discover our own as we relate to, differ from, imagine, argue with, and feel emotions or think thoughts that were evoked by the poem.

It is in that spirit that these poems have been collected. A Minnesota poet has written each of the poems in this volume. Each poet was born and lived for some formative time, now lives, or worked for many years in Minnesota. You will therefore find some local idioms and expressions. You will also find wonderful poetry that has no home.

In 2005 my father died. One day in late May of that year, I walked into a shop in my neighborhood and was startled to see Father's Day cards. My knees buckled. I instantly realized that I would have no Father's Day card to send that year! A ritual of many years had been altered forever because of Dad's death. My grieving surfaced again. Returning home, I began to write about that experience and my reactions to it. I also read poems about fathers and sons. Words, as often had been the case, helped me deal with this disruptive change and grieve my loss.

Elizabeth and I hope this book will serve similar purposes and more for you. Some readers will be encouraged by a poem found within to write their own account of loss. Some others will find in the poems in this volume sources for solace, challenge, metaphor, hope, or tears. Read. Use the poems and pages that follow for grieving and for renewal!

The Wind Blows,
The Ice Breaks

 *Prelude*

Susan Williams

THE POET SAYS GRIEF

The poet says grief
never leaves only changes, it
waits outside doors, keeps a place
at the table. Hides in a high room
with mirrors to the wall, flings
from the attic to the roof of the mouth.
Whispers at windows.
Slips out with the smoke.
Creeps eave to eave like a grin.

Gathers with night in the trees when we
won't let it in.

Louise Erdrich

GRIEF

Sometimes you have to take your own hand
as though you were a lost child
and bring yourself stumbling
home over twisted ice.

Whiteness drifts over your house.
A page of warm light
falls steady from the open door.

Here is your bed, folded open.
Lie down, lie down, let the blue snow cover you.

Kirsten Dierking

FOR THE DISAPPEARED

At recess once I was playing tag,
running away from the other kids,
when I opened my eyes, I was
lying face down in a far corner
of the empty schoolyard, I never
really knew what happened.

How easily the continuous thread
of our lives can be broken. The
missing pieces we never get back.
The dark spells we wear like a veil
to our last moment, not knowing,
not ever understood.

Jude Nutter

from MEDITATIONS: TYNE COT CEMETERY, YPRES

2

The world is indifferent, but the heart never can
be indifferent. Don't ever tell me
there are too many poems about the dead: the dead,
among whose ranks we shall one day number, outnumber
us all and should be given their due. Remember.

Linda Back McKay

THE ART OF GRIEVING

No art is perfect and that is why the art of grieving is practiced at all.
This class is mandatory for matriculation into the next life,
which may or may not contain grieving. Either way, you take
your chances. When presented with no choice, drop to your knees
and lower yourself to the floor. Prostrate, let the tongues of despair
wash over you in morning sunlight. After you are tired of being
on the floor, pick yourself up again. Wash your hands in the bathroom
sink with a strong soap that foams, you will notice, like malted milk.
Above all, do not think about grief or it will take hold and squeeze
harder than you can bear. Take to clouds instead. Clouds like these,
that swim about the stifled river, skirting daytime and night time,
neither coming nor going in their chameleon lives. Take
yourself on a journey to somewhere small because big
is impossible right now. Save big for when you are stronger.
In your apart place, watch for the least of things – a thimble,
a fluff of dust wafting across the desk. The old quill pen
that you can now use to scratch a message home, *please
await my return. Your humble servant,*

*The wind whirls
around us …*

Larry Schug

WINDSTORM

In the eye of the night I lie awake,
half afraid, half in awe of the wind
penetrating every crack in my being.
I think of my brother and his wife
in the next town downwind,
open-eyed and clinging to each other
as the wind that mocks everything
to which we think we're anchored
roars through our lives.
I see them leaning in the gale;
how tightly they must be holding each other –
like roots gripping the soil,
as my brother's cancer blows away his time,
minutes flying off like shingles from a roof;
and I hear the cry in his wife's heart
drowning even the howling outside their walls.
I roll closer to my own wife this night,
circle her in my arms, desperately.

Eugene McCarthy

COURAGE AT SIXTY

Now it is certain.
There is no magic stone,
No secret to be found.
One must go
With the mind's winnowed learning.
No more than the child's handhold
On the willows bending over the lake,
On the sumac roots at the cliff edge.
Ignorance is checked,
Betrayals scratched.
The coat has been hung on the peg,
The cigar laid on the table edge,
The cue chosen and chalked,
The balls set for the final break.
All cards drawn,
All bets called.
The dice, warm as blood in the hand,
Shaken for the last cast.
The glove has been thrown on the ground,
The last choice of weapons made.

A book for one thought.
A poem for one line.
A line for one word.

"Broken things are powerful."
Things about to break are stronger still.
The last shot from the brittle bow is truest.

Mary Willette Hughes

Even So...

When I tell his story,
       long entangled in my story,
will words be shards of glass
       that arrow and wound him again?

When I tell our story
       to his circled brothers and sisters,
will they want to draw back,
       rise, leave my Thanksgiving table?

When I tell our story,
       a bridge of truth across the page,
will others decry my public
       poems of private pain, of recovery?

Even so...

I am compelled
       to bring winter and summer rain
to the desert land of prodigal
       hearts who will enter the story,

who will carry our lives home
       and hold in thirsting, cupped hands
the possibility of new life,
       poem by poem, page by page.

Diane Glancy

THE INEVITABLE

Strange how the long shadow in the family
photo points straight to her. The sun
coming down upon us in the farmyard like
a spotlight we try to get away from. But
not her, bold, grinning, standing out
from the group a bit, as though she is
not afraid of the black finger that seems
to pick her out.

See the wire in the corner of the picture,
my brother says, it is just the shadow of
a utility pole that makes a dark trough
across the bare yard to her.

Her eyes shine like ponds in the field –
her certainty that our lives sprout again
like new grass.

We look silently at the album.

I would like someone to talk to – perhaps
the gas station attendant who worked to
get bugs off our windshield after a trip
to the farm, the station sideways on the
corner – then we could lean out the window
and say to him – there's a chance our mother
is dying.

Monica Ochtrup

LOST

When the sun went suddenly under, with the wind pushing hard, I
remembered that Saturday in March when I was nine and tried to get
lost. It was with Cornelius's house showing up for the fourth time that
I finally gave in, decided on the front door, and asked if they didn't have
any cookies for me. I told Cornelius what I'd been trying to do. I didn't
know him well, but I knew he was too young to be in a wheel chair, and
that my father went to his house to cut his hair. So Cornelius told me
that day, because I asked him: What happened? I wasn't sure I should
ask, but he had laughed so hard when I told him about trying to get lost,
I thought it would be all right. And it was. I couldn't figure out how, though.
How could it be all right with Cornelius that Army doctors used a spinal
to put him under when he got wounded; that the wound healed, but they
were only beginning to learn about spinals and how they worked, and
it worked wrong for Cornelius the rest of his life. I kept a sadness after
that. In a town that size where the same houses show up every day, the
lives in every one of those houses become part of your life, in some
unspoken way. It happens every day. And you can't get lost.

Richard Solly

One Morning Cereal

One morning, cereal. The next day, cancer.
Instantly from appetite to deprivation.
Lightning sears the sky without warning. Affliction
can't be negotiated, though even Jesus pleaded
with his father. It's the one undoing we all share.
When it comes, we are not the same.
Only later, much later, when the inflamed sky
subsides, when I swim back to the far shore
of ordinary life, when the long irradiated wave
has passed, now traveling on through someone else,
do I shake the dark water off myself
and wonder if I'm better for having arrived
on sand when others drown. I peel away
my sodden clothes so the sun can touch my body.
"I'm still here," I say, but I am not impressed
that the swim was so far, so long.
Whom do I thank? No one. I take no credit
for my survival, nor do I shake my fist.
I taste the salt on my lips, the smear
of it a kiss, intolerable and lovely at once.

Carol Pearce Bjorlie

AMBUSHED

Just this side
of the Paul Bunyan State Forest,
a Showy Lady Slipper hidden by fern
startles, poses
dangles her pink toes.

Sometimes a word comes
or a whole line, and a poem transcends
like a double-rainbow in my rearview
mirror

Then there's the routine
mammogram surprise.

Pam Wynn

Epilepsy: This Is What I Know

epilepsy is characterized by seizures
that have no known cause

seizures   like sharks
travel   with great bursts of speed
dwell in the depths
of the ocean   or near the surface
in coastal waters   or far out at sea

they see well in dim light
easily detect
the smallest electrical field

seizures like sharks circle
I feed them daily
a steady diet
of yellow pills

they are swift   mysterious
I respect them for this
and never swim alone

Marilyn J. Boe

A Strange Thing Happens

A strange thing happens when a clot fires into the brain
wipes out bridges of memory, washes away what's familiar.

Nurses run with your gurney, bag air into you,
until the respirator sighs against your blistered lips,
your body a funnel for fluids changing

with the current of computers, your room a weather station,
you the pulsating center of a serious storm,
dark clouds I watch night after night.

Months later you wake up, and I tell you we have a new grandson,
both of you unable to remember the dark months of sleep,
both of you reflecting my smile with a bewildered look.

Nancy Frederiksen

Speech

in memory of Charles A. Elkin

After four months in a coma,
he starts trying

to move his mouth around in
painful efforts.

He seeks re-entry into this
earth world; he seeks it

because he is as afraid of
that other world as we are of

his survival chances in this one.
We are all on edge.

He lies there twitching; mumbles
out. Everyone is excited.

Unexpectedly, every so often,
his leg jerks up to his chest.

Every once in a while a word
comes out clear,

"Shit."

Alex Lemon

Ashtray

When the paramedics kicked his heart
back to life—the blooming light, doctors
cutting away his vocal cords, a lung—
Grandpa heard children tearing
through leaves. I promised not to tell anyone
about the flowerpot filled with ash,
the yellow-walled smell. I caressed his back
with a warm washcloth. Vibrator at his throat,
he buzzed his pleasure. Kneading skin
in silence, I traveled the universe
of his tattoos. Mountains and ships—acres
of faded ink. I rubbed circles, pushed
until his back roared, the ocean of his gravel-
skinned shoulder blade where a woman,
naked and fierce, dangled from an anchor,
winking her secrets: there is never a reason for fear,
simple as the crashing wave—Grandpa's smile
as tumors turned him slowly into night.
How he held the X-ray to the window,
inhaling a cigarette through the hole in his throat
until it blazed, bright as an eye.

John Berryman

DREAM SONG #172: YOUR FACE BROODS FROM MY TABLE

Your face broods from my table, Suicide.
Your force came on like a torrent toward the end
of agony and wrath.
You were christened in the beginning Sylvia Plath
and changed that name for Mrs. Hughes and bred
and went on round the bend

till the oven seemed the proper place for you.
I brood upon your face, the geography of grief,
hooded, till I allow
again your resignation from us now
though the screams of orphaned children fix me anew.
Your torment here was brief,

long falls your exit all repeatingly,
a poor exemplum, one more suicide
to stack upon the others
till stricken Henry with his sisters & brothers
suddenly gone pauses to wonder why he
alone breasts the wronging tide.

Susan Deborah King

Twinges

Once you've had cancer, ever after
every odd sensation is worms
beginning to nibble you.
Jabbing pains, persistent aches
or coughs, cuts slow to heal can be
a witch's finger poking your flesh
to see if you're fat enough yet for the oven,
can be a choking piece of poisoned apple,
a spindle's prick casting an evil spell.

How to trick the witch, get the weight
of her own ego to throw her*self*
into the fire instead, how to
enlist the assistance of dwarves
and princes for rescue. Before,
death was a fairy tale that would
never actually happen to us.
What liars our parents were!
The bogeyman is *too* real!

That's not just the pounding of our hearts
when we discover another questionable
mole. It's him on horseback,
his hoof beats aiming our way
to scare right into us, living hell.
We stick out our tongues, bare claws,
make like gargoyles, trying to protect
this sanctuary of our blood and breath
and drive off the monster another little while.

Ruth Roston

PLAYERS

Early October, maple trees
burning the air. Kirsten
leaned on her rake, said
she was dying. Spoke only once
the Greek names for dying.
She hoarded her words for our game.

Scrabble. Like fiends
every night she was home
we played Scrabble.
Kirsten dazzled the board
with words she had pried
out of doctors, technicians,
and SYZYGY (using two blanks)
and ZYGOT and LUMPH.

Alphabets entered her veins,
dripped letter by letter
through bottles, through tubes.
The score of our games
in her hospital room
was charted like fever.

Home in May. Maple seeds
ticking the screen. Kirsten
spelled BLACK (going across)
and BURY (going down)
made SADLY made SHADOW,
accused me of letting her win.

Kirsten won, dizzy
with maple seeds falling,
with hundreds and thousands
of words in her cells,
in her veins, with SADLY,
with SHADOW . . .

Norita Dittberner-Jax

CROSSING

In Memoriam
Don Belleau

Now I see how the living begin
the passage: Information
arrives, the measured cadence
of bad news, an announcement
as sudden as the warning
on the loudspeaker, "The store
will be closing in five minutes."

If you sleep, you remember
with your first breath upon waking;
you weigh yourself, but what use
is the scale, artifact of an earlier life?

You live out your days amid the clocks
and calendars of earth, but your mind
is on the old verities,
death, truth.

Those who love you bear this,
watch as you lay aside one object after
another, wristwatch, gloves,
the contents of your life taking on dignity
as you sweeten into your passing.

Mary Kay Rummel

CAMOUFLAGE

Egret walks the river bank,
eases toward the water,
eyes fixed on something moving,

darts, nibbles, winds
her serpent neck and cleans
feathers that radiate a scent

of white. All layers, patterns,
shading invisible to my eyes.

Like her, I glean and gather
all that lies before me,
even my decline.

I swivel my head,
missing the spot behind,
where my ending waits.

One morning will I touch
my face and find it smooth
as river rock,
no eyes to see?

Jim Moore

It Is Not the Fact That I Will Die That I Mind

but that no one will love as I did
the oak tree out my boyhood window,
the mother who set herself
so stubbornly against life,
the sister with her serious frown
and her wish for someone at her side,
the father with his dreamy gaze
and his left hand idly buried
in the fur of his dog.
And the dog herself,
that mournful look and huge appetite,
her need for absolute stillness
in the presence of a bird.
I know how each of them looks
when asleep. And I know how it feels
to fall asleep among them.
No one knows that but me,
no one knows how to love them the way I do.

Mary Kay Rummel

Symbiosis

There are spaces in old trees
                that open   into other lives
spotted choral orchids
                live on fungi at their roots
almost
but not quite parasitic   after flowering
                their tiny capsules nod.

Is it like that in me?   Almost benign?
And how does the seeing affect it?
In the way a partial eclipse is seen as blood on the moon?

After fifty years bark buries fire scars in old trees.
The shape I see in my breast during the ultrasound
looks like basalt, eroded in the center,
a place for something to settle. I remember
my mother's scarred body, burns still raw
when cancer killed her. I turn away from both pictures,

think of the coniferous forest
              wolf lichen covers every trunk
cones hang
              like long fingers from the sugar pine,
soft   insides like flesh
              a deepest scarlet.

Michael Walsh

OVERDUE

Amounts due massing like flies
to his name, my father said,
I must smell like meat. Sunburned
arm stretched across the table,

he asked God to chop. His fist
hit formica like the butcher's blow.
My startled arm swooped beneath.
Don't worry, he said. *The numbers,*

they're morphine. They fill you silly
before you're ever born: blood tests,
due dates, birth weights. Don't worry,
kid, they won't collect for years.

But I understood systole, diastole,
checked my wrist for the sound
of numbers louder than my name,
darker than the dollar's ink.

Patricia Kirkpatrick

The Black Squirrel

After she cleared the empty
breakfast glasses of chocolate,
swept up the rash cereal from the floor,
she took her notebook, wanting
to say how it was at this moment.
In a few weeks she would take her mother
for surgery. She would sit with her sisters
in a room filled with cushions
the way they did when they were girls,
almost wetting themselves in fear of
the removal of a musical chair.
Inside the hospital they would wait
for their mother's heart,
coarsely opened,
to regain a sinus node.
Her children, at home, would get their own
breakfast. Now that they were older
nothing was the occasion
it had been, when, while she buttered
toast, wiped hands and faces,
one of them would run to her shrieking,
"The black squirrel's in the side yard
digging up the tulips!"
A slash of fur through the grass and the bulbs
she set in earth
like prayers were taken.
Her mother, she hoped, would heal.
The children, she knew, would go.

Margot Fortunato Galt

Late Song

for my mother

She's breaking my heart
after years of glazing and firing.
"My pretty one. You're my pretty one."
Old lady of trembly lips and thin hair –
"My baby. You're my baby."
Her stubbly chin rubs mine.
We kiss good-bye.
"How far away? How far?"
She points to the wheeling birds.
"I tell the birdies you'll come back."
In these last days, there is
no real life apart.
The broken
heart knows
its spill
of joy.

Robert Bly

LOOKING AT AGING FACES

for Bill and Nancy

Some faces get older and remain who they are. Oh
You can see disappointment there, where parent-
　　teacher
Meetings have affected the chin; or the nose got
　　pushed
To one side by deaths. So many things happen:
People moving away, or your mother becomes crazy
And bites the nurse.

Each face had a long time in the womb to decide
How much it would let worldly things affect it,
How often it would turn toward the wall or the
　　woods,
So it didn't have to be seen, how much
It would give in, how stubbornly it would
Hold its own.

Some faces remain whole and radiant. We study them
To find a clue. Aunt Nettie said, "My father
Put on cufflinks every day." Memories like that
Help. One face, as firmly profiled as a hawk,
Used to say: "The world is fair, and if it's not,
I think it is."

For some of us, insults sink in, or the feet
Inherit two roads and lose the way; for others, cold
And hunger come. Some faces change. It's not wrong.
And if you look carefully, you can see,
By glimpsing us just after we wake,
Who we are.

Phebe Hanson

CRONE

Carefully supported by my sturdy walking stick,
carved by an old Norwegian in Lutsen, I pick my way
down the incline to where waves crash against rocks,

settle myself against a sun-warmed stone that just fits
my body, gives respite for my stiff back. I spread
and lift my billowy skirt to let sun rest tenderly

on winter-paled legs, bend to examine
closely skin on knees and calves,
scored with fine wrinkles I can hardly believe are there,

preferring to believe my legs are unchanged since
childhood, legs hanging happily from monkey bars or
bicycling down country roads as I look for pussy willows.

Lame Deer says our bodies get so wrinkled as we age,
that we begin to look like the rocks themselves and the markings
on my legs do look, I think, like the ones on these ancient
                    glacial rocks,

a thought I find strangely comforting. "Soon I'll be a crone,"
I say to myself, "an elder filled with wrinkles and wisdom,
and when even my walking stick can no longer

support my old body, I'll slide down the path, a gleeful
child again, crawl on the rocks like a baby new to the world,

toward crashing waves and endless sky."

Lucille Broderson

EIGHT OF US

Brought Mother jars of crocuses,
stole the neighbor's watermelons,
forgot to hoe the corn.
Whirled our waists on the school's iron fence,
exposing our panties and petticoats.
Smashed our dolls, then howled
with the broken pieces in our hands.
Fought over the wishbone, wouldn't eat the neck.

Father shook the brothers,
rapped his knuckles on their heads.
Mother muttered and rubbed
our sunburned backs with vaseline.

We thought we'd last forever,
but we grew long and brittle
and split like fluff on dandelions.

Johnny left first, there was nothing here to hold him.
Then Mary dropped laughing in a parking lot.
How like her, that big booming woman.
But dishes piled high in her kitchen sink,
the dogs unfed for days.
Then it was Liz, always up first in the morning,
finally too slow on a busy street.

The others wrinkled and shrank, sagged
in their chairs, afghans on their knees, eyes huge behind thick lenses.
In pairs they left, two in one year,
two in the next.

Now I'm the last,
of all those faces around the table,
all those bodies warm in bed.

Alvin Greenberg

as we, too, grow older

suddenly all the parents have taken up dying,
this one of several cancers, that one by the heart,
by stroke, my own father of forgetfulness: one
by one the parents moving back in with the children
and the children feeding them, often by hand,
getting up at night to take them to the bathroom
as day by day the parents recede from the world
the way the world recedes from my father's mind
who once traveled it as if he owned it all
but now lets it slip through his fingers
like his shoestrings, not remembering what's
connected to what, or how, the great loop
of his life coming untied and he can't recall
what goes where, wanders out with laces loose
and dragging, stumbles over them, of course,
on the top step, plunging downward, arms out,
where we, who saw this happening, catch him,
he floats gently into our arms, laces trailing,
almost as if there's no one there, yes, as if
he's forgotten how he's weighed on us all these years.

Annie Breitenbucher

Worth

There will come a day
when he no longer remembers me.
When the look that I crave, that
one instant of soft flicker and smile
will be gone.

He will introduce me as his son,
and he will mean it.

There will come a day
when I question the value
of these silent visiting hours.
And so, now, I rehearse:
It is clear, I will say,
there is worth. It is all clear

today

when I am not
my father's son.

Nancy Frederiksen

Broken Bones

She has broken her arm, tripped over a throw rug
by the back porch door near the painted cupboard
where she keeps the turkey roaster.
She wants to go to the nursing home.
We do as she says. Check her in.

Quick to give orders, she now takes them.
We see dependence grow like a shadow.
When her 97-year-old roommate talks
about having a baby, as if she could,
Mom sees this as a sign—time to leave.

She checks herself out and at home,
practices lifting her arms,
inch by inch, day by day.

Home-care workers come to the house.
She tells them to dust
where to find the vacuum.
Just exactly what to do

with those throw rugs.

Gail Rixen

His Mother

She still refuses to go,
lives on muffins and jelly
and that confused marmalade of hers.
She forgets him in mid-sentence
and leaves for something sweet
put up years before
without leaving her chair.

He asks doctors how she survives
with all the wrong ingredients
to his recipe.
When he comes with firm intent
and a moving truck,
she isn't fooled
and tells her rocker
"I won't be back."

Ted Bowman

SOFTEN THE BLOW

for Bertie

The Alzheimer's came first
Later came the stroke
Robbing her diamonds and pearls
She lost the past
And her left side
She lost the stories she loved
And her mobility
Still she smiled
No matter what
"I love you"
"Thank you, dear"
"I'm just glad to be alive"
And affirmed us
"You're a handsome fellow"
"So good"
"Your hands feel so warm"
She loved us all
Grandchildren, nurses, friends

A smile can soften the blow
Especially so a genuine love of people
And of life

No doubt there was grief, loneliness, and fear
But those she kept in a plain brown wrapper
Not for public display
Allowing her smile to fill the room

It makes your dying harder, Mother
And easier
Our tears blend with smiles
Grief and unexpected joy overflow.

Nolan Zavoral

Young Blond Guy at Piano

Who played after lunch, surrounded
By wheelchairs in the nursing home where
He was rehabbing from a car crash, and who
Would stay a titch under a month, and unfurl
Flapper and big-band ditties because he
Sensed the ache in his audience, and who
Once called up my mother as a duet partner and
Filled behind her melody line to *You Gotta See*
Mama Every Night (Or You won't See Mama
At All). Her grasping, spidery fingers worked
Their way along some ancient motor-neuron
Path, and impressed the staff, who called me, who
Called her, who said, "What young blond guy?"

Annie Breitenbucher

SILVER SPOONS ON GLASS

She offers her love in spoonfuls of ice cream.
Two hours, at the nursing home, every day;

a ritual of feeding
that is not about hunger, but faith

that she is meant to be with
him until the sun sets.

Lifting vanilla, fresh raspberries to his lips
she fills a holy silence with all that cannot be said.

Fifty-eight years, seven children, their life both rich and hard –
all of it spun down to the ice cream, her kiss

his smile. From the vow never to part all heartache
has been wrung. Never has it been as simple as this:

he loves her, she loves him. The sun sets to heaven's
song – the sound of silver spoons on glass.

Lucille Broderson

WILD GEESE

Once they led my car as it curved the lake,
their shadows long on the hood.
Once they appeared on shore without a sound,
slipped in the water as I swam by.
I moved toward them, not raising a ripple.
I didn't see them lift or skim out of sight:
one minute, the leader's black eye stared,
the next I was alone.

Now when I hear the wild geese cry,
I know I'll see them soar from some hidden bay,
turn, and circle slowly over my head.
I'm like stone then, but as they swing away,
I laugh, and stretching tall as I can,
I call them back.

One day, they'll hover above me,
their white tails fanning
like a sigh as they settle around me,
the warm wings nudging. And then, that urgent whisper.
Come, it's very late.

John Engman

THINK OF ME IN D MAJOR

I know everything I know about dying
        (all doctors do
        is hope and cut)
from what I've been told by my own soft brain
while waiting in a waiting room:
                "Dying

seems to be something living organisms
        do naturally.
        You might be next."
I'm waiting for a doctor to check my pulse
and draw blood. I feel sick, not dying,
                but scared,

and poor Johann Sebastian Bach is trying
        to comfort me
        in D Major,
soothing with high strings, then coming in low
for a few notes, as if to say,
                gravely,

"Maybe you think about dying too much.
        Why, even you
        could live and be
swept away by a dose of baroque music."
The doctor who examines me agrees
                with Bach,

reducing all my intimations of mortality
     to medical facts,
     psychosomatic
muscle spasms and gas pains. I am alive,
but the prognosis isn't good: someday I will
     be dead,

and even the doctor admits that he can't find
     one cell
     of my soul
with his silver instruments and microscopes.
It's hard to believe that anyone can live
     hopefully

if the body is simply a score written in red
     and white counts,
     brainwaves, x-rays.
But harder to believe that anyone can die
when Johann Sebastian Bach argues
     for the soul

in D Major, a symphony of goosebumps.
     Maybe what dying
     organisms call
living is learning how to be swept away?
I admit that I feel swept away, somewhat
     immortal,

with Johann Sebastian Bach in the air.
     So, if someday
     I disappear,
just think of me as a goosebump, or a note
that disappears in D Major, swept away,
     but still here.

Leslie Adrienne Miller

SUNDAYS WHEN THEIR LAPS WERE FULL OF LIGHT

What is this familiar yellow stuff at the glass again
but Sunday's wide gold loops made by two parents,
two children, driving in a blue Buick away from church
to the meal the children always choose:

a baked chicken leg, yams in syrup, milky pudding,
then the long afternoon of the small town. Laps full
of sunlight, they drive past the courthouse, the banks,
the closed Woolworth's. They cross the river on a steel bridge.

For the mother, they drive by every house for sale in the rims
of town, long low houses hugging lazy sun-blond lawns.
The father later drives past what he likes, fields
where glowing sheaves lean on the light. One of the girls

in the backseat collects the way it falls in her lap, breaks,
falls and breaks again: phone poles go shadow, shadow, shadow,
and trees go shadow, then shadow, shadow, light light light.
They ride in what the parents surely think is pleasure.

The mother wants other houses. Bigger, prettier houses.
Further out. The father would like to hear his music now,
Beethoven which is at home in a stack of plastic 45s,
but this is the middle of the century and of the country

where even on Sunday there is no Beethoven on the radio.
There is a word, once applied to an herb, but now
obsolete, that some would like restored to the language:
anacampserote...that which brings back departed love.

Of the two girls in the backseat, only one,
in thirty years, will wonder: Did we lose the word
because we failed to believe, or did we fail to believe
because we lost the word? The other will not

wonder such a thing but have a child and a house
in Kansas that the mother, now grandmother
wanders with sigh of approval. Carpets thick as grass,
a rumpus room that always gets the morning light.

That which never arrives cannot be lost, is what
the mother would say to the other girl. She would
say, without ever having read Alain, *Desire is far
inferior to love, and maybe, does not even point
the way to it.* The father, after Beethoven, would
not say that, but neither does he know what to do
for his other girl, the one that he suspects of never having
loved at all. This is the light, she thinks, that promised

everything in shadows dropped into our laps, lavish light
that mingles what we hope for with what we think we've lost.

The ice cracks
beneath us . . .

Heid Erdrich

PHOSPHORESCENCE

At the end of love, disaster
sucks all the air from the room,
swings shut doors in our brains' corridors,
hums down like power failure,
switches our skin off.

At the end of love we find a Quaker island
where surf by night breaks glowing
with foam. Tiny creatures whose bodies
make their own light fill the water.
We two strangers wade to the shore,
our own forms lit by the moon.
We wash ourselves of our old, other lives.

Then the crushed-shell beach-path
confuses itself with the horizon of large
white stars hanging so close to the island.
At the end of love, we lose
our balance in a globe of glowing points.

When we reach to steady each other,
low clouds begin to trail above us
in shapes of peaceful spirits.

Jill Breckenridge

DRAWING OF MY FAMILY: AGE 6

One cloud above a white house,
one mother, a little girl,
a father sitting in his blue car,
as the cloud rains under itself.

In my childhood drawing, a sidewalk
reaches from the front door to a road
where the car drives away.

Black smoke curls out of the chimney,
black V birds flap away from the tree,

the blue sky doesn't leave, nor the mother
in her red coat with twelve buttons,
all of them fastened, even the one

under her round head, turned away
from the father and daughter.

The windows wear capital-R-shaped curtains,
and the doorknob is colored black,
drawn big enough that a good father,
if he forgot the key, could open
the front door and come home,

but if it's night and he's the bad father,
he won't be able to see the doorknob
until tomorrow when the good father returns.

A gray cat should be colored in, hunting
mice to hide under the kitchen table,
and a red cocker spaniel, old and fussy,
biting company because his ears hurt.

The little girl should be running
across the yard yelling, "Hurry up!"
to her baby brother, not in the picture
because he isn't born for three more years,
but she misses him already.

It should be raining all over this picture,
not just under the single white cloud,
raining on the mother in her red coat
until she looks toward the little girl,

raining on the father's car until
he stops driving and walks back
to stand on the green strip of yard

with the mother and daughter,
so they'll all be smiling big smiles,
way up above their ears,
like they already are in this picture.

Stanley Kiesel

DORIS

Eyes filled with underweight
Expressions, and a pin in her voice.
Discovered her in my class
One day, stuck like a piece of
Gum, to the bottom of my shoe.

She, one of too many children
I know, so politely mangled it
Makes me mournful to teach;
Sexless, glassy, a tuneless little
Sample for the Kodak ("say cheese").
Retiring more and more into her
Skin eruptions. Today, sent to me
In a peacock dress, she will not
Paint but remains crouched in
A corner, crushed, like a pack animal,
Beneath a mother's ribbon.

Spencer Reece

from ADDRESSES

iii. To My Brother

the postman circles with his thick blue sack
a school bus streaks the horizon with orange
carrying with it the shrieks of adolescents

someone is being teased someone is imitating
what it is like to be retarded to be handicapped
someone is shoved for being a homosexual

down the street the AA meeting starts up
in a church basement a coffee urn thumps
a wounded chorus unfolds their metal chairs

a retired stewardess with thick red lipstick
speaks of her umpteenth hospitalization
the clock empties its chest of sixty more ticks

another year passes still no word from you

Roseann Lloyd

this child

this child is about to be touched
touched funny told to shut up

about the fast lesson down   how
if you rub a nipple   it sticks out

hard   this child is about to hide
her nipples inside her shirt   inside

her undershirt this child is about
to be forced to do without

a father   hurts too much
this child is about to cry at his touch

about to run and hide
this child is about to be deprived

of childhood   it's all shut up
this child is about to be touched

by the power of a man who lies
who will disregard her cries

call her *seductive/beautiful/slut*
this child is about to give up

clothes silky to the touch   hide
her nipples inside her shirt   this child

will give her childhood up
her own tentative touch

her imagination playing free and wild
the daydreams of a child   this child

will be gone at his touch
offered up   shut up

Sharon Chmielarz

AFTER THE DANCE

Mom was a pretty woman.
She couldn't help it if men
asked her to dance.
Dad was the disciplinarian.
When they got home
he hit her and washed her
dark hole out with soap.
He was a hard man,
the scissors I plunged at his back
couldn't go in.

John Caddy

Touching

The clothesline hums with fear.
The boy watches from the corner of the house.
The man is going to beat the dog,
ears flat and withers shrinking,
who can never believe this is happening.
All of them are living in their throats.
The man is red, the boy is pale,
both are trying not to cry.

The boy is caught within another laying on of hands,
at the cabin when they cleared the brush
and the wheelbarrow piled with branches
was too much for him, when the birch turned switch
and laid open his skin.

The dog presents his throat and yelps again.
He grips his forearm where
the scars lie white across the tan.

Philip Bryant

THE FIRST CHRISTMAS AFTER THEIR DIVORCE

Coming home
for Christmas
after their divorce,
though it wasn't
final yet – as if anything
really is –
I could have died
to see my mother's
things taken away
and in their place
a space as empty
and windy as any
western plain.
My father tried
to make small talk
but that didn't
go far. It started to
snow, so we went out
to buy a tree and
brought it back
and decorated it.
I remember the
red, green, yellow, and
blue lights, how
they once enthralled
me in the middle
of the night as my
sister and I woke and
tiptoed into the
living room.

The presents
arranged under the tree
shone like smooth rocks
under a clear stream.
Now my father
shrugs it off,
makes light of it,
but the dark spaces
grow under the
branches that flex to
the breaking point
with tinsel and ornaments
my mother,
in her haste to leave,
didn't bother to take.

John Calvin Rezmerski

SECOND MARRIAGE

He divorced his wife
and married whiskey,
and forgot how to fight.
He spoke less than before,
    "How are you, neighbor?"
barely remembering the names
of old friends.

After his wife left,
he began to take long walks,
some of which he came back from.
Strange little bruises
appeared on his face,
and cuts on his fingers,
and he limped as if
kicked in the shin.

Whiskey was beating him up;
unfaithful whiskey,
who had whispered
such words of love,
didn't understand him.

Carol Connolly

Divorced

I am alone,
single,
solitary,
celibate.
I have borne eight children.
I worry now that I will die
a virgin.

Caroline Vogel Marshall

I Dream the Divorce Is Final

It is spring and early morning. I am loping in slow motion
up East Avenue to my mother's best friend's house where
the women are drinking coffee, wearing a pink nylon jacket
that billows when I peak before I drop back to the balls of
my feet. I pass my lawyer mowing his grass. He nods and
keeps going back and forth, up and down his even rows. The
hard lines are gone from his face. Mrs. B comes out to the
porch door to draw me in. She takes my hand and presses
it flat between hers and says, "I'm so sorry." Behind her the
women glance around anxiously. Some repair their lipstick.
All their mouths are moving. I can tell they are grieving for
me, my daughter, my mother. They look only at each other
and their pocket mirrors. They do not see my pink wings or
the rhododendron breaking through the branches.

William Reichard

In Florida

There, amidst the malls and kosher delis,
I wasn't measuring up. He'd taken me
to meet his family, and I, farm boy
from the frozen north, made mistakes
when I ordered at restaurants;
lost my temper at the mall.
His grandmother didn't approve.

He'd been asking me to make this trip
almost from the day we met.
We traveled in June, not the best time
to head south. All retirees possessed
of any common sense were headed north,
their minivans in caravans moving slowly
up the interstate. The first day, I burned.
I'd been watching an ibis in the condo
parking lot, amazed at a bird I'd only ever
seen in hieroglyphics on Egyptian tombs.
Stick-skinny legs and that impossible beak!
As I stood on his grandmother's balcony,

I could hear her inside her refrigerated den
saying
>   *he seems nice but it isn't right,*
>   *those people can be so cold*
We broke up shortly after that. It was nothing
he did or said. Only, a growing chill when
we were together, my way of being in the world
that collided with his. The last time I saw him,
we were both crying. It was August. Dog days.
The heat, unbearable. It was a bright morning
but I was cold, even in the sun.

Spencer Reece

INTERLUDE

We are two men on a park bench
in Palm Beach oblivious to the two men

who start their truck with that boy
from the bar inside dragging him

in the dark to the fence strapping him
with a rope to a post in Laramie,

Wyoming, where he freezes and dies
over five days. My dear, it is late.

The Flagler museum is shut.
Stay with me. Remain here with me.

Mark Vinz

The Fear of Loss

All his life he was afraid of something. He was always the last
one out of a restaurant or theater, checking and rechecking
all the seats and tables for whatever might be left behind. He
opened the drawers in motel rooms, moved the furniture
and beds. He made duplicates of everything he wrote, and
whenever he went to the store he bought two of each item just
in case one should get lost.

The older he got, the more his fear grew. His houses were
filling up, he was repeating everything he said. When he
became ill, he refused to see a doctor—he simply had too
much to lose. When he died, deserted in the end by wives and
friends, no one came to the funerals, and now, not even his
children know the locations of his graves.

Todd Boss

DON'T COME HOME

ranks first among
the worst things
someone you love
can say. Not even
the common *I*
hate you does
the damage *Don't*
come home will
do. You can live
with *I hate you,*
same as you live
with the past.
You abide it. *I*
hate you in fact
can be worth
coming home to,
like anything built
to last. *I hate you*
may be the mythical
two in the bush
the bird in the hand
is worth, while
Don't come home,
by contrast, is
that first bird,
caught bird, scared
to sing its song,
percussive wings
held fist-fast just
so long.

Kirsten Dierking

The Pleasure of Safety

That, in the course of justice, none of us
Should see salvation: we do pray for mercy;

Portia, *Merchant of Venice*
William Shakespeare

I imagine it down to the shoes
I'm wearing on the witness stand.

A faceless defendant. A quick
conviction. Bars and chains.

How this didn't happen. He was
never caught. So I also imagine

an eye for an eye. He breaks in
my house and this time I'm ready.

I've got a gun. I'm going to kill
him. First, I give my testimony:

For all the days I've been too
afraid to leave the house. For

nights I can never spend alone.
For the time I woke up kicking

and clawing the man I love,
hearing your voice call me bitch.

For sheets soaked in adrenaline
sweat. For walks I can't take.

For thinking I must have deserved
your touch. For crippling years

of heart-sick fear that made me unsure
which way I should point the gun.

Now that he's here, I know
who's to blame. I aim for the skull.

Pull the trigger. Watch his head
blown the fuck apart, his blood on

the walls like a proffered flower
of red appeasement. It makes me

smile. You know this is not
who I wanted to be. But late at night,

startled by every noise in the house,
this is the ending that guarantees

sleep. I *crave* good sleep. Don't
count on mercy from women forever.

Meridel LeSueur

DEAD IN BLOODY SNOW

I am an Indian woman
Witness to my earth
Witness for my people.
I am the nocturnal door,
The hidden cave of your sorrow
Like you hidden deep in furrow
                and dung
            of the charnel mound,
I heard the craven passing of the
                 white soldiers
And saw them shoot at Wounded Knee
                 upon the sleeping village,
And ran with the guns at my back
Until we froze in our blood on the snow.

I speak from old portages
Where they pursued and shot into the river crossing
All the grandmothers of Black Hawk.
I speak from the smoke of grief,
             from the broken stone
And cry with the women crying from the marsh
Trail and tears of drouthed women,
         O bitter barren!
           O bitter barren!
I run, homeless,
        I arrive
        in the gun sight,
           beside the white square houses
        of abundance.
              My people starve

In the time of the bitter moon.
I hear my ghostly people crying
                    A hey a hey a hey.
Rising from our dusty dead the sweet grass,
The skull marking the place of loss and flight
I sing holding my severed head,
                    to my dismembered child,
A people's dream that died in bloody snow.

Joe Paddock

Earth Tongues

This seething earth
everywhere writhes up
into tongues
of life, each telling
a perfect story
which ends in death
again   and again
and again . . . .

James Lenfestey

Driving Across Wisconsin

September 11, 2001

Do the trees know what has happened?
Is that why that one's crown
is rimmed with fire, that one's arm
droops a flagging yellow?

Sumac, thick as people
on a crowded street,
redden suddenly from the tips.

Ferns in dark hollows of the forest
reveal their veins.

Bouquets of asters, purple and white,
offer themselves from the side of the road
to all the wounded passing by.

Ann Iverson

WHEN A SON GOES OFF TO WAR

I walk out into the world alone at dusk
watch blackbirds with no strategic plan,
mission, or vision gather in the naked tree.

Hundreds of them fly in this impromptu session,
where they put their wings together and form
an arc of shadow, a coalition between light and dark,
while from branches, decisions scatter in the air.

Filled with privilege like never before,
I open myself to the visual world
where doctrine and creed do not matter
so even God finds himself amongst

their turning eyes looking West,
knowing everything we long to know
about how light ends
and darkness finds its way.

David Mura

Hope Without Hope

Words on the page, prayers, even shouts of rage,
What do they count against tanks, missiles, guns?
For each line that you write, each war you wage,
Ten thousand hands write reams to drown your one.

No matter how beautiful, pungent, pure,
In that cacophony, your poems are like roses
Tossed on an ocean of thunderous azure;
Washed in the gutter by a dozen hoses.

Okay then. Nothing could be more utterly
Useless. History rolls on, lie by lie.
You, in a world of greed and cruelty,
Who offer us poems, well, tell me. Why? Why?

Tim Nolan

For My Country in Its Darkness

But it seems as if there's light —
on the television screen — behind
the e-mails — and from the dashboard —

everything is lit — in full sunlight —
but then there's sudden darkness — as if
someone put drops in your eyes —

and said — "See how everything's so nice" —
Even the rooms for torture are lit
like drugstores — with shelves and shelves

of choices — "We could do this to you —
or that — it depends on what you say" —
And our fear is so well lit —

that it almost seems like no fear —
because the sky is blue — the waves
roll in their regular course — while

the trees grow to the height of the house —
it seems as if there's light —
but nonetheless — we are in darkness —

Wang Ping

Tsunami Chant

I'm not a singer, but please
let me sing of the peacemakers
on streets and internets, their candles
in this darkest moment of night,
their bodies on the steps of government buildings,
their voices from the roots of grasses and trees,
from the well of conscience, voices
that refuse to be stamped out, extinguished.

I'm not a prayer, but please,
please give my voice to the children
in Baghdad, Basra, Afghanistan,
and every other bombed place on earth,
their crying out in pain, in flesh and wraith;
please give my hands to the mothers
raking through rubble for food, bodies,
my sight to the cities and fields in smoke,
my tears to the men and women who are brought
home in bags; and please give my ears
to those who refuse to hear the explosions,
who tune only to censored news, official deception.

I'm not a citizen, but please
count my vote against the belief
that American way is the only way,
count it against the blasphemy of freedom,
against a gang of thugs who donned crowns
on their own heads, who live for power
and power only, whose only route is
to deceive and loot, whose mouth moves

only to crush, whose hand closes
only into a grave.

I'm not a worshiper, but please
accept my faith in those
who refuse to believe in painted lies,
refuse to join in the chorus of this supreme hypocrisy,
refuse to see you, to let their conscience sleep,
wither, die. Please accept my faith
in those who cross the bridge for peace,
only to be cursed and spat upon, but keep crossing
anyway, every Wednesday, in rain and snow,
and my faith in those who camp out night after night,
their blood thawing the frozen ground,
their tents of hope in this bleak age.

I don't possess a bomb, don't know
how to shoot or thrust a sword.
All I have is a broken voice,
a heart immense with sorrow.
But please, please take them,
let them be part of this tsunami
of chanting, this chant of awakening.

*The ice breaks,
the wind blows . . .*

Thomas McGrath

NEWS OF YOUR DEATH

for Mac Blair

First, a stunning numbness
Like touching a live wire…
Or the shock of reality entering through my broken arm
When I fell from a house…
The smell of the snake just before the rattle…

Then: the feeling the fish has
The instant the dynamite explodes
Just under the thick ice.

Phebe Hanson

CURLS

They told me,
the women who came
bearing macaroni hot dishes:
You must look nice
for the funeral.
They took out the long
curling iron, plugged
its cobra-skinned cord
into our current,
rolled heavy straight strands
around the hot cylinder's mouth
until my long hair
sprang out alive and curly,
frantic corkscrews bobbing
on my puffed sleeves.
But I pulled away
from their soft hands,
ran from them to the sink,
poured palmfuls of cold water
through my curls until they hung
on my neck and I was plain enough
to bend and kiss my mother's hard lips
as she lay in her coffin.

Lucille Broderson

In The End

All that last day at the cabin,
the lawnmower held you up, you
who could barely stand.
You rammed and rammed the mower
into the raspberry thicket
until we had lawn
where we didn't need it,
didn't want it.

That night, holding your night pail,
your hand went limp. The warm yellow
flowed onto the pine floor, between the planks.
Your teeth clenched. You wailed, a high keening wail.

Once the sounds that came from your lips
were words. When you'd nick a finger
or bump a shin, you'd glare at me, say,
I'd better not get really sick,
you'd never be there.
Then the cancer grew in your brain
and each day you became less and less,
and I was there. Surprised, but I was there.

You were my little boy then, feet wide apart,
rolling around the house in a toddler's gait.
How I loved nuzzling your neck,
squeezing your shoulders. For days
I lay in your arms, sobbing.
You held me tight, your eyes wide,
no change at all on your face.

Ethna McKiernan

ELEGY AGAINST THE DYING OF THE LIGHT

for Steve Arhelgar

After shock passes,
grief and anger still remain –
for your bright blond hair
scarred by red blood,

for your talents cut mid-air
hanging slack now, inert –
for gunshot crack
that wasn't accident,

for a grand slam ending,
home-plate harder than stone
growing by the river flats
where I see you yet –

for the sheer waste of it,
the universe still streaming sun
and you, Mercedes man,
old companion, steady con,

hired by your own laughter
sparking like July 4th fires
gone awry in dark,
you've finally fallen

under, not a tender bone
left nesting
in your shattered head –
damn you, praise you,

friend: I loved you
and you're dead.

Beverly Rollwagen

SHARING

You know that song "Sometimes I Feel
Like a Motherless Child"? Well, now it's true for
me, I am one. And so is my sister. My sister, who
did all the hard parts connected with our mother's
death, including choosing the coffin and what
she would wear, and getting the lipstick she liked
over to the funeral home. Also going over to the
hospital to see the body at four in the morning,
so when she called with the news, inconsolable,
which made me the same way, we spoke (when
we could speak) about how there's no doubt that
the spirit (if that's what we have) of our mother
was gone. What she left was her shell, which was
bathed and dressed and curled and brushed so that
she almost looked like herself again. But when I
touched her, as I had to, holding my sister's hand,
loving that they got her hair right and the scarf
draped over the folds of her neck, loving that
my husband and children were there, loving my
sister and her husband and their children and
grandchildren, who finally relaxed and ran up to
the coffin peeking in and saying goodbye to
greatgrandma, then I finally felt how solid death is,
how large a space it needs. I've cleared out a room
in my life to contain my new guest, and since my
sister and I share custody of the loss, we pass it
back and forth with great tenderness, taking care
to share equally, as our mother always wanted.

Alvin Greenberg

c=the physics of farewell

nothing we know can exceed the speed of light,
but death, i think, can carry its cargo off
almost as fast. remember einstein's rocket?
life and death are the famous twins, and no matter
how many times we perform this experiment,
i am the one who is always left behind,
growing older, waiting for your return.
far away you go and fast, and the farther
and faster you go, the younger you'll remain.
often at night when i see you, i can see how well
the experiment works: your skin so smooth, your hair
still fine and blond. yes, the experiment works; it
proves nothing more than itself, but damn, it works
and you are further and faster away than ever
and einstein, once again, has been no help.
i understand everything now that's worth understanding
about time and distance. soon i'll be fifty. still
the experiment runs. i don't think i'll be here,
dear twin, for your return, but lucky's the world
that you'll be bringing your youth and beauty back to.

Sharon Chmielarz

Joe

There's a coldness about us
as you lie in the casket.
We're a stiff-armed people
shaking hands

to hold off a kiss

We look at you in the parlor
your face full of bandaids
but you can't fool me:
I see the hole where the bullet
entered your forehead.

There's a bad-mouthed silence.
There's mewling in the corner.
There's a smile on your face –
you got your boots

out from under our table.

Florence Chard Dacey

Widows

After she had cried
a tubful of tears
she lay in it for three days.
(Because she was overweight,
a little splashed out
on the children's faces.)
She had to take deep breaths
and go under and got so
she could submerge twelve minutes
at a stretch, time enough
to review his life and theirs
caught in the bubbles she released
and which seemed to continue their flight,
breaking through the surface tension.
Her children hung over the edges
and tried to catch them,
but they wouldn't break.
She imagined herself out beyond
the earth's pull watching them float past.
Somewhere up there he waited.
Perhaps he would prick them, break the spell.
Only then could she escape this womb,
surprise her children, geyser up,
a plump glistening she-serpent.
Why, in a few weeks she might
even wade up town,
greet the other new widows.
They would stand for hours
facing each other
like freshly washed windows
or babes just awakened
from the long dreamless nap.

George Roberts

lament

my old red schwinn had a carrier on the back fender
on your first day gail i would ride you to school
you would hold my side with one hand and balance
our lunch sacks in the other your legs dangling
outside the flashing spokes   we would talk and laugh
if it should suddenly rain i would give you my jacket

but by three years old your heart had grown too large
for your body i never rode you on my bike i
never took you to school   i am afraid to go there
myself now and my heart is the reverse of yours
sister it is growing smaller

Pam Wynn

MISCARRIAGE

A woman in a white, sleeveless dress
Printed with small daisies

Her hair pulled back
In a rubber band

Opens the door
To the empty house.

Her husband parks the car
In the garage.

The woman sits
In the new Boston rocker.

The window box
Is on eye level.

She stares at the purple
Pansies about to open.

"One in five ends like this,"
The doctor said.

"You're young. There will be others,"
Her friends said.

Her husband hesitates
As he enters.

The woman stands,
Slowly walks to the bedroom,

Places the white
Crocheted blanket, the yellow

Booties, the tiny knitted sweater
In a clear plastic bag.

Freya Manfred

THREE CHRISTMASES AGO

When she ate chicken the grease ran on her mouth,
And grey hair twisted at her temples in a light sweat;
Her nose was firm and smooth and young;
Her eyes were grey, or green with giving things away;
Only the plants could not love her,
She watered them too much, they lost their roots;
With her crooked walk she bent and watered and bent.

> But her Christmas cactus pink and pointed touched
>   my heart,
> And in all the blue bulbs gleamed a fire;
> In all the bulbs she swung with sagging arm skin
> And old unrimmed glasses and little and laughing.

My grandmother was a long-grassed hill;
She was water in a cup too trembling full
So that we had too much of her;
She was made of the same pink fire
That lit the veins of our Christmas cactus and made it sweat
    with love scent
In the room with the fire.

> And now she is covered with snow:
> The long-grassed hill is covered with snow;
> Five trees grow there.
> She has walked her crooked walk to bed.

Dying Old and Dying Young

In the picture
they sit
almost touching
forever
married
straight
as spring rain
as corn rows
as knives in the drawer.

She is the second sister he married.
They buried the first in bridedress forever
embracing her baby. Her picture
hung in the front room
fifty-two years
faced the rocker.

Rocked
in all seasons, locked
in the blinkless line of her eye,
startled
forever.

Nancy Paddock

ASLEEP IN JESUS

the old cemetery at Morton   the final
resting place of pioneers
after they had broken
the sod
thrust their roots into the tangled
web of ancient grass

a tree   carved from pale sandstone
a leafless monument   bearing
only words
an amputated stump
of loss unbending
the family tree

its branches scattered on the ground
like bones
with the names of children:

      Daniel   born 1881
                     died 1893

and Benjamin   1884 to 1902

    "Asleep in Jesus, blessed sleep,
    From which none wakes to weep."

awake, unweeping Gunder Lind dug stones
that worked up in his wheat fields
every spring   for thirty years
dug stones and buried
sons

till he had plowed the prairie
black   opening
its darkness to the wind
carving deep   his grief:

> *"'Tis hard to break the tender cord*
> *When love has bound the heart.*
> *'Tis hard, so hard, to speak the words,*
> *Must we forever part?*
> *Dearest loved one, we have laid thee*
> *In the peaceful grave's embrace,*
>
> *But thy memory will be cherished*
> *Till we see thy heavenly face."*

"O blessed sleep
from which none wakes . . ."

at fifty-two, unyielding Gunder Lind
fell down
weary of the hardness he bore
out of the ground

tears still break
out of these stones
washing down the furrowed names
dissolving
even the hardest

leaving this tree
that they may not go
unmarked   into the ground
these pioneers
who dropped their seed
into the darkness
and bore
its fruit

James Wright

THREE STEPS TO THE GRAVEYARD

When I went there first,
In the spring, it was evening,
It was long hollow thorn
Laid under the locust,
And near to my feet
The crowfoot, the mayapple
Trod their limbs down
Till the stalk blew over.
It grew summer, O riches
Of girls on the lawn,
And boys' locks lying
Tousled on knees,
The picnickers leaving,
The day gone down.

When I went there again,
I walked with my father
Who held in his hand
The crowfoot, the mayapple,
And under my hands,
To hold off the sunlight,
I saw him going,
Between two trees;
When the lawn lay empty
It was the year's end,
It was the darkness,
It was long hollow thorn
To wound the bare shade,
The sheaf and the blade.

O now as I go there
The crowfoot, the mayapple
Blear the gray pond;
Beside the still waters
The field mouse tiptoes,
To hear the air sounding
The long hollow thorn.
I lean to the hollow,
But nothing blows there,
The day goes down.
The field mice flutter
Like grass and are gone,
And a skinny old woman
Scrubs at a stone,
Between two trees.

John Calvin Rezmerski

Elegy for Spectators

Facing someone else's death
in the back room of a respectable place
is no time to feel a fever.
You measure the temperature of your mind
in sins above normal,
there is quick significance
in the length of your bones,
you match one leg against the other,
listening for pains in the marrow.

A corpse says nothing about agony,
less about a vague ache in the throat.
The other visitors among the flowers
seem to hear something you missed.
They pass it along: life goes on, life goes on.
The murmur echoes back from the lilies
so softly only you hear the change:
goes off, goes off.

THE WOMAN WHO WAILED

the woman who wailed
    in the grass, in the spring
    wailed on the hill
    on her knees in the spring
the woman who wailed
    with the sound from her knees
    with the sound coming out
    from her belly and knees
the sound ripping out
    spilling life on the ground
    on the blanket of sod
    newly placed on the earth
wailed at the grass
    laid across the bare earth
    fit into the rectangle
    cut in the ground
tore with her fingernails
    into the roots
    of the barrier sod
    between her and her child
crouched on the hill
    with the rushes of sound
    choking on phlegm
    in the wails in the grass
the woman who wailed
    unable to stand
    grinding the daffodils
    under her hand
the woman who wailed
the woman who wailed

Michael Dennis Browne

DREAM AT THE DEATH OF JAMES WRIGHT

The wind is rolling the buffalo down;
the wind is shining and sharpening the buffalo
and rolling them down.
The sheep have already scattered
toward the forest,
sheep are streaming
along the stained edges of the forest.
But the wind is rolling the buffalo down.
We have not built a shelter for them,
we have put up no corral.
They don't know enough to
come together, bind their black fur
together, sit out the storm.
I see one huge one struggling
inside a lantern of grasses.
The wind is rolling the buffalo down,
shining and sharpening them
and rolling them down.

Robert Bly

SNOWBANKS NORTH OF THE HOUSE

Those great sweeps of snow that stop suddenly six feet
        from the house...
Thoughts that go so far.
The boy gets out of high school and reads no more books;
the son stops calling home.
The mother puts down her rolling pin and makes no more
        bread.
And the wife looks at her husband one night at a party
        and loves him no more.
The energy leaves the wine, and the minister falls leaving
        the church.
It will not come closer—
the one inside moves back, and the hands touch nothing,
        and are safe.

And the father grieves for his son, and will not leave the
        room where the coffin stands;
he turns away from his wife, and she sleeps alone.

And the sea lifts and falls all night; the moon goes on
        through the unattached heavens alone.
And the toe of the shoe pivots
in the dust...
The man in the black coat turns, and goes back down the
        hill.
No one knows why he came, or why he turned away, and
        did not climb the hill.

Anna Irena Sochocky

Time Between Hours

For three days and three nights the wind did not blow
I did not dream but lay in bed listening to coyotes singing
off-key in the cattail reeds and cornfields.
The wind has gone out of the farm because Dad
isn't here, you said. But on the day of the funeral, a breeze
like a faint exhale came over the slough, pushing dense heat
through our lungs, around corners of the house until our muscles
ached with longing. Details hung in the air like humidity.
Hymns. Scripture. Flowers. The suit. Death keeps you busy.
There wasn't any time for photographs of your father
clutching dead pheasants, their marble eyes staring absently
into blue sky. No time to consider the smell of grain dust
in the air at twilight or the reasons why it is good
for the earth to lie fallow, to rest sometimes. But later…

time between hours lengthened…
…and soon there was a little more time to talk
about combining at midnight and watching Sputnik satellites
make patterns in the North Dakota sky. More time for stories
about prairie blizzards and hunting feasts, finding arrowheads
buried in the black earth, and your father's memory of seeing
bands of Lakota traversing the landscape.
As the days passed, there was more time to remember
the way he once stood, one hand in his pressed Levis,
the other one low on his sweetheart's waist
as if it were a first date not a 50th anniversary celebration

…and still there would be more time for the stain
of red wine and the precious taste of a fresh grief
to settle on our lips.

Gerald Vizenor

Haiku in English (selections)

Time plays in silhouettes
    Like empty swings
      Moving in the wind.

    Winter shore
Everything leans away from me
    Shaped by the wind.

    Apple blossoms
The world troubles me again.
    Fury of the wind.

    Every day at the lake
Our footprints are washed away
    Remembering a friend.

Jean McKenzie Johnson

ECHOES

I don't remember remember remember
echoes echo.
I don't remember white wool carpet
black wheels
carrying his body
    through the door, red lights shouting exit exit exiting.

I don't remember
his last day
frantic knowingness,
wheels spinning forward.

White fish on white plate,
pale berries on cereal
black seeds of hope floating in bowls
blue plastic, red blood,
a silver bell.

I don't remember the cherry wood box
shiny polished lavished gloss
white duck pants
boating shoes on bare feet,
we sailed the waters of Florida.

Today, I don't remember his dying.
But I heard a sighing breath, saw him leave
    out to the starry sky, the galaxy where he lives.
It was morning, Sunday morning, and
the sagamore fled, the little fishes fled and
he was gone, too.

Elizabeth Bourque Johnson

FROM ROOM TO ROOM

Each night I touch the foreheads
of my sleeping children.
Deep among the bears and blankets
Julie stirs as I breathe over her,
inhaling her warmth.
I tuck her foot under the covers,
leave the night-light on.

Open Tricia's door to dark and silence.
Step over unfinished Monopoly.
Sixth grade - the long thin body
growing under the comforter.

At Stephanie's door I knock and wait.
Sixteen is not sweet.
Headphones on, floor strewn
with jeans and notebooks.
"Night, Mom. Close the door." That's all.

Kris's room.
No forehead here to touch.
All her clothes hanging in the closet,
shoes side by side.
The silver crucifix.
A corsage drying by the mirror.

Georgia A. Greeley

BODY BUSINESS

My mother said, "Marie told me she decided to have
breast reconstruction so her husband wouldn't
feel like he was hugging a man." I had just taken
off my shirt, my chest still bruised, the steri-strips

just starting to detach. My twenty-year-old daughter
walked into my bedroom without knocking,
saw me, and bolted out the door,
letting go a long "No." A month later

she said, "That's not so bad."
My youngest brother asked, "Is it legal
for you to walk down the street with your
shirt off, now?" I picked up six-week-old Ted,

my dispatch partner's son, to still his cries.
I pulled him to my chest, the first child I'd
cuddled since my surgery.
Ted didn't care – he snuggled right in.

Deborah Keenan

COMFORT

*"We have everything we need to believe
right here in front of us."*

— Dabney Stuart

I put my mouth on the wound of the tree.
I breathed, a child in my father's yard.
My breath was a Valentine, came from my red heart.

The tree lived long past the time of its wound.
My father went to his grave, and I believed in his death.
In the yard I would do his work, taught my children his name.

My mother inside the window watched us
and we turned to wave, her love for us involuntary,
streaming through the glass; she held her position.

My oldest son said, high in the branches of the tree,
"Here are his arms, I am swinging from his arms."
The tree turned to me, promised to live until I could do

without him.

John Berryman

Dream Song #207 – How are you?

– How are you? – Fine, fine. (I have tears unshed,
There is here near the bottom of my chest
a loop of cold, on the right.
A thing hurts somewhere up left in my head.
I have a gang of old sins unconfessed.
I shovel out of sight

a-many ills else, I might mention too,
such as her leaving and my hopeless book.
No more of that, my friend.
It's good of you to ask and) How are you?
(Music comes painful as a happy look
to a system nearing an end

or an empty question slides to a standstill
while the drums increase inside an empty skull
and the whole matter breaks down
or would it would, had Henry left his will
but that went sideways sprawling, collapsed & dull.)
How are you, I say with a frown.

Patricia Hampl

from RESORT - PART II

Something was wrong? Went wrong?
>   *My life broke in half.*

You're sorry?
>   *Sorry for myself.*

You're looking for some sort of answer?
>   *I thought I was supposed to furnish those.*

Came here to find direction?
>   *I'm contemporary under protest. Could we call it a rest, a*
>   *rest before a new beginning?*

Whatever you say. Was it love?
>   *It was.*

Ended badly?
>   *I said my life broke in half.*

You're of an age for that.
>   *As people say when there has been a death.*

Feel free to talk about it, won't you?
>   *This is, all this.*

But – forgive me – we can count on you not to go on and on?
>   *What brevity there is in a wave and in the pigment of the*
>   *rose! These are my subjects.*

Bill Meissner

The Dance of the Ripples

The Saturday evening after Dad's funeral we find ourselves
        at the lake,
and Mom wades alone into the calm, darkening water.
Deep in grief, her skin is the color of silt. Concentric circles
move out from her thighs. The small ripples
hurry away from her, travel the distance
to the shore and reach us, her children,
who stand still, ankle-deep, unable to talk,
        the humid blanket
of dusk weighting down our shoulders.

At this lake tonight, everything
seems too quiet or too loud, rising or falling, moving or not
        moving.
One of us exhales with a soft hiss.

We watch her wade into deeper water, up to her waist,
        though
we all know she doesn't swim.
But it's her heart we worry about now, her small
red heart drowning inside the twilight of her body.
I want to call out to her:
Not so deep, not so deep. He's not here
to steady you when you step
into the drop-off.

Suddenly, music wafts through the screen of the pavilion:
Glenn Miller's saxophones roll smoothly toward us.
Mother faces the center of the lake.

Forgetting for a moment, she sways side to side to the
      rhythm,
sending out small sudden waves that glisten in the
      moonlight.
It seems as though someone should ask her to dance.
Then she closes her eyes, silencing the music
while the ripples clasp their rings
tightly around her waist,
holding her, holding her.

Jim Moore

from SEVEN INVISIBLE STRINGS

I.
I remember my mother toward the end,
       folding the tablecloth after dinner
            so carefully
     as if it were the flag
            of a country that no longer existed,
   but once ruled the world.

Warren Woessner

THE DISAPPEARANCE OF MY FATHER

He is fading
like the head–lantern of a lost miner
who breaks through a wall with his last strength
and finds, not air and light,
but more tunnels
filled with gleaming people
who move too quickly to follow
and use a constantly-changing language
in which every other word
means good-bye.

Ted Bowman

Male Tears

Tears well up and seek surface drainage.
Blocked by poor priming,
Clogged pipes,
Inexperience,
Rocky soil,
They reluctantly return to their storage place
To await a plumber
…or a handyman.

Michael Dennis Browne

Neighbor In May

my neighbor is hammering
and mending his house
he fixes in almost a frenzy
by night he dreams of his wife
dead nearly a year now
he dreams of nailing and healing
he dreams of repairing the damage

Betty Bridgman

Companioned

We climbed across the crusted field
and broke a thin drift on the hill.
Over whatever fences reeled
by wood or road we went, and still

only a little tired – a mile
of Winter is worth five of Fall,
but with your hand at every stile
I could not think it hard at all –

so long as I could cheerfully
look ahead, above, below –
but not behind me, lest I see
only two footprints in the snow.

Mary Willette Hughes

CREDO

> *...thorns should never be*
> *plucked from the roses.*

– Ellen Key

I am alone
and before me
on the theater's wide screen,
in time-lapse photography,
a tangerine rose discloses

its delicate morning sky,
sculpting the horizon
petal
by petal
by mortal petal.

Closed in the darkness
of dying and death
my horizon is empty.

But before my eyes,
as color and shadow
slowly unfold,
I encounter the heart
of the rose.

I begin to open,
begin to comprehend
as new tears form,
the days of sweetness,
the days of thorns.

Thomas McGrath

REMEMBERING LOVES AND DEATHS

They happened in us...
But later we moved away –
Or they did.

Went west.
Went south to the goldfields.
Disappeared somewhere beyond Salt Lake or Denver –
Their roads are still in the map of our flesh:
Easy to get to almost any time
Around midnight.

But the land shifts and changes, the map
Gets out of date,
The century stretches its joints,
And one day we stand by the marked tree and ask: WAS IT HERE
WAS IT HERE
While, stunned but tireless,
Memory, the lodestone that always points toward pain,
Hunts, slow and sluggish for its North,
Turning through the thickening crystals of tired flesh
That was pure honey, once.

Kathryn Kysar

ANOTHER POSTCARD FROM CHINOOK

The wind on the prairie moves
straw-like grass. It undulates
against the crackling dry air.
It is not winter.
She is in the attic inventing
the whispering ghost of her father.
In the almost aching silence,
the movement of birds outside the window
shatters the peaceful madness,
but the light can't break through
the tattered shades,
the piles of forgotten pink insulation.
She climbs down the broken, creaking
stairs to stand and face the prairie.

Su Smallen

CRENELLATION

As our brains fold
into themselves to create more surfaces
for more knowledge,

our hearts, too, fold
into themselves. We call it breaking.
Hearts never break.

They fold in to create more surfaces
for more love, or
else they cease.

Our hearts sit on
top of our diaphragms. Something floods. Our hearts,
a fist reflex.

Breathing shallows, can't support our clavicles,
our arms. We hang
off plumb. We fall

into our innermost. Some straps there do not
let go. We're like
moon-tagged egrets,

flooded from nearshore to shore. The more diluted
a remedy,
the greater its potency. As our hearts

crenellate, we
feel what more we could have done, we could have said
then, when our hearts,

though good, were smooth.
Now we are more capable, now we find more
ways we could have

loved you. More ways
we love you now.

Madelon Sprengnether

from ANNIVERSARY

2.

I lied a little. There are things I don't want to tell you. How lonely
I am today and sick at heart. How the rain falls steadily and cold
on a garden grown greener, more lush and even less tame. I
haven't done much, I confess, to contain it. The grapevine, as
usual, threatens everything in its path, while the raspberry canes,
aggressive and abundant, are clearly out of control. I'm afraid the
wildflowers have taken over, being after all the most hardy and
tolerant of shade and neglect. This year the violets and lilies of
the valley are rampant, while the phlox are about to emit their
shocking pink perfume. Oh, my dear, had you been here this
spring, you would have seen how the bleeding hearts are thriving.

David Wojahn

Fort Snelling National Cemetery: St. Paul, Minnesota

Thirty thousand dead, the markers all identical,
and with a map I find his stone,

                       find my own name chiseled
here between the monoliths of airport runway lights
and "the world's largest shopping mall," its parking lot

nudging the cemetery fence. The spirit in its tunnel
does not soar, the spirit raised by wolves.

The parable of the cave, the spirit raised
by shades and flickering shadows.

                            Down the grid

of colored lights a Northwest triple seven
lumbers into sleet

                that melts against my father's name

like the striking of a tongueless bell, a code
compact and unabstract as DNA, and with my hand

I trace three times the rough, wet letters.
The jets shriek

                and the rain-slick marble shimmers.

Evelyn Klein

TORNADO COUNTRY

Tornado country this –
Not to be fooled
by sunshine
or calm
when thunder rumbles
in the distance –
Life goes on as usual
between storms
Most times the funnel
only sweeps by
the sound of a train
or explosion
when it strikes
splattering a lifetime –
Rebuilding is slow
love becomes
mother to apprehension –
It could happen again –
It is only a question
of time

Bill Holm

from THE DEAD GET BY WITH EVERYTHING

V.

Who do the dead think they are!
Up and dying in the middle of the night
leaving themselves all over the house,
all over my books, all over my face?
How dare they sit in the front seat of my car,
invisible, not wearing their seat belts,
not holding up their end of the conversation,
as I drive down the highway
shaking my fist at the air all the way
to the office where they're not in.
The dead get by with everything.

 *The sky begins to blue ...*

Mary Logue

BLUE

The ones we love—
the dead—
hover above our heads
like balloons from
a day at the fair.

Our love is the string.
The sky, —well, you know
what the sky is,
endless blue,
all that is promised.

We are afraid
we will forget
what it was like
to have them in this life.
We clutch at the string.
We are children.
It has been a long day.

But if we realize how long
our love is, if we realize
how big our life is,
if we can see how blue
that sky would be with the balloon
right in the middle of it,
we would let go
and walk away.

Heid Erdrich

The Widow's Grove

Drinking sleep I grow old—
on and on I push through the grove
to a declining orchard
still putting out pale buds.
Trees step into rows.
Faces flicker in the boughs,
familiar, dear, those long gone.
Just when one seems in reach
it's the tree's white sprays
I find in my arms, unfolding
against me, tight with hard pushes
that have not forgotten desire.
When I turn to the marsh
they branch out after me,
but they are not my husband who,
when loving was not enough,
gathered me, sinking, from sleep.

Marilyn Benson

GOOD-BYE

> *Say that I have found a good solution*
> *and am on my way to the roots.*
>
> — Wendell Berry

Saturday we said good-bye to our father.
Upstairs, we stand around a bed
And open the plastic bag of his ashes,
Feeling the thick gray grit,
About four pounds.

Some we save in a wood urn,
Ladling with a measuring cup.

Still too much to fit the bronzed box.
He was a big man.
We squeeze to make it fit.
One last hug, someone says.

At the Baptist cemetery we sit in the shade,
Tell stories about the immigrant farm hand
Who bought a farm,
Sing Swedish songs, laugh, cry.

My brother digs the hole.
We lower the box with rope Dad braided.
Dirt on the box, sod on the dirt.
Singing *For the Beauty of the Earth.*

Sunday while our mother goes to church
We carry the wood urn through the fields.
Twelve of us, children and grandchildren, taking turns.
At the center of the farm
We throw his ashes into the strong south wind.

Kate Green

At Total Eclipse of the Sun

In this strange dark at noon,
through the false light of the world,
we see the dead, forgiven, float like dim fumes
from under the parked cars.

So they have been traveling
with us all this time –
Grandmother gone before I knew her
as anything but a soft row of buttons.
Gone on a Christmas, my father said.
The cherry light of the ambulance
blinked as her heart did not,
tree lights pulsing tinsel.
Grandfather fainted against the mirror
into his own reflection. I heard
his skull on silver glass.

John dove into heaven from the motorcycle
on a mountain blind curve.
Barb eaten too young by cancer,
her skin caved in.
Even the cat shrunk to bone in August dust,
breath stopped like an old fan.

The dead are with us.
They borrow the blue between trees.
And we never had to miss them,
only the smell of their clothes
was gone, only the hair
stuck in their combs.

One by one,
great clear birds of the wind,
they greet our hearts and empty streets,
our dishes in the sink. They bow
to our little hours made and counted by the light
that disappears.

Tenderly they remember our hunger
for sugar, our breasts, our open mouths.
Our leaves gone red blood back into water,
back into fire.
Back into dirt.

E'ireann Lorsung

POEM FOR YOUR BROTHER

He should have had this day
when it has finally stopped raining
in New Hampshire and things
are green, and along the new-paved
road to your parents' house cherry
trees are in single and double
bloom, and the last cold
has gone from the brook, which runs
as ever diagonal and downhill,
away. You would want
this for him, the smell
of your father after cutting wood,
even ache in your right shin where one
log sprang back from the axe
and struck bone. Flight
of crows out of high branches,
tin cans disintegrating. And years—
His hair curling and brush-
thick and black, who once held
you upside-down underwater, who
chased girls and loved sound
of skateboards, trucks, I think also
the feeling of his nephews' skin
and their breath. This all ought to be
for him, small blue flowers nameless
by the roadway, mountain
covered in leafed-in trees; his heart's
good, your brother, who yelled
at Christmas, who was your mother's
favorite, who lived alone and left

the television loud so someone
would wonder, call the super, so
it wouldn't be your mother finding
him. When the rain comes again all
of you will be under the grey roof
with the skylights; in the mornings
it will seem fine until you remember
and, outside, an oriole, misplaced,
will pull six thin notes from air,
bend the branch orange
and black—there is no going
back, despite every should:
it will fly away.

John Minczeski

GRANDFATHER JANOSZ AND THE POLISH GRAVES OF NEW PRAGUE

With neon from the bar lighting the snow
that swirls past my knees, it looks like
I'm walking through the ground
halfway among the dead taking it easy
zgoda, zgoda, above the earth and below.

Seven languages he racked up
knocking from country to country.
Four of them he spoke well
and they all boiled down to Polish.

That spring when Ned brought a box of dirt
back from Poland, we baked the living crap
out of it first, then sprinkled it,
grey powder, over the graves.

An old lady grabbed my hand to kiss.
Her Stanley, she said, was home now, at peace,
repeating the Polish *zgoda*, peace, peace.
All that weeping, but it was only Poland.

Ethna McKiernan

GRIEF

The way it comes from nowhere,
lapping at the half-healing heart
like a dog hoping to be loved
if he just keeps coming by to play.
Then later like a needle,
a high thin pain, the body
twisted double with it,
utterly undone.

Suddenly at a traffic light
someone walks exactly
as your mother walked,
that stoop, the slow look left
and right, the long coat
swishing below knees. Frozen,
your mind won't let your foot
release the clutch, and you're reeled
in again. Grief.

How long a memory lasts depends
upon so many things: the ruby shade
a rose can glow in August
and how it hooks you back
to her garden; whether or not
one of the boys had a fever
that Sunday morning when you
took the call; how much
alcohol or solitude can do; how little,
in the end. But grief, that thief,
softened by time or abandoned
with intent, doesn't budge; it is the one
constant that outlasts them all.

Deborah Keenan

Blue Heron

We arrived carrying our usual human trouble, hoping to walk
Those troubles deep into the forest, hoping
To leave them there. Not as burden for the forest, knowing
All too well the forest and its beautiful indifference.

At the dam I looked left to a hidden curve of creek,
Joe looked right to the still water past the small island.
Blue Heron lifted from the curve, her wingspan almost
Touched us, and she landed past the island, bowed to eat.

Right after my mother died, eight years ago, I saw Blue Heron
In this small valley; I knew then my mother had left
Her exhausted body behind and slipped into this
Winged disguise. I was happy for my mother's new life.

We've searched these eight years for one more sight
Of Blue Heron. And in our sorrows this day, three times
We saw her take flight, three times land, three times lean
Into shallow water for food and reflection. *She's gone,*

I said to Joe. We carried the sight of her back to our city,
Our hearts strangely stirred and strangely at peace,
Her extended wings visible against the green of spring.

Connie Wanek

THIS WINDY DAY

I warm my hands on my coffee cup
and think of my father
lifting floundering sow bugs
out of the swimming pool.
If he had a tiny towel
I think he'd help dry them off.

When we lived nearby
he'd visit on his bicycle
a bag of oranges in his basket
and he'd hold one up – a miracle!
How could a tree do this?

Clouds warm their hands
on the rising sun, then move off.
Families of clouds don't necessarily
stay together.

This windy day
the children and I go walking
through streets deep with leaves.
We talk about Grampa, how we miss him.
But children feel things differently –
swift, sharp, a side-ache.
Then they're running again
shoelaces untied, leaving us behind.

James L. White

Submission to Death

Our loved ones, allowing them to die forever
like noticing the weakened sun in late winter.
Sometimes we let them go through dreams,
giving away their clothes,
keeping only the pocket knife or star quilt.

'Do what you have to,' we remember them saying.
And so we must do with them
who are tired from their effort to be dead,
still not sure where to go,
so they linger with us awhile
before their journey.

Sometimes we sleep well in the midst of terrible grief
or remember something funny they said.
They give these small gifts to us before they leave.
Then for no reason, months later,
we walk into a room unexpectedly filled with flowers
and cry totally, knowing they are dead and forever.

It's good.
Our weeping lessens their memory of us
and they begin to travel more easily,
doing their work, which is to be dead,
not for us or anyone.
We feel better just speaking
of the past,
that too without them.

Ed-Bok Lee

AT MIHWANGSA TEMPLE

Nothing today but a girl
who flaps the wooden rafters
calligraphied on a silk-white ribbon.

A red candle some cold fingers lit
to memorialize her early death.

Bronze bowl of fresh figs
and black flies. Fertility
unnerved.

Someone remind the wind
everything is already swept away
in the afterlife.

And wonder
like a flame's grace
should possess no weight.

Who she was.
What anyone does to slip
through evening's mask of trees.

A strange lust, this life.
Everywhere beautiful souls
bathing in grief.

Cary Waterman

After a Death

Your death recedes like a bad storm,
a sudden one with boiling clouds
the color of ash
that roll out to sea
across water which turns from turquoise
to ink
to blue-green again.

For weeks after you were gone,
you were my first thought on waking,
the mother who had left me where I stood
abandoned on the beach
looking out over a sea where
white gulls circled and cried.
Each day I swallowed that knowing
first breath of morning,
my body snapping in a whiplash.
And then the painful pull away,
the way the placenta tears from the mother
to make two labors, two births.

But today your absence
plays a softer melody.
Colors of morning blend together
in yellow and white.
It is spring.

A cat jumps to the window
to watch the hungry sparrows
which are you now.

The cat. The birds. The morning sun.
It's all you.
And this sky, cloudless,
your high forehead stretched,
wrapping its blue around everything.

Cary Waterman

The Unread Book

It comes toward you when you least suspect it. You are on a
busy street in a foreign country and no one is smiling and you are
unsure of the language and the clouds are grey and from every
direction mothers push children in strollers who are all crying
because they are hungry or bored or sad and you step into a
bookshop because it has finally just begun to rain very lightly
and you see the unread book you gave your mother the Christmas
before she died and you walk over and crack its spine.

Patricia Barone

from THE LIFE IS GREATER THAN THE BODY

Before he was sick, he began
a poem, lying on his back
in the middle of a gulley wash road
that snaked the woods all night.

As he lay upon the sand, he collected
small sounds, the breathing of deer,
crepitation of twigs or bones.

◆

The body of work John left
is small. As his body
grew smaller, his thumb print,
water mark, was raised
from the days of his life,
                compressed
then expanded like the stock
of his handmade paper—into the most distinct
layers: that camp with his father, found
by moon and compass, the way
martial arts he learned were something more
                than balance—
a fulcrum,
an enduring presence.

Richard Solly

WHEN I DIE

for Rose

If my cancer returns, and I'm chauffeured
to Paradise in a limousine, and you live that first night
on earth without me; when after midnight,
standing at the window, you see the room floating
in the trees and the sky spongy; or when lying in bed
yourself like a ghost, animated by the clanging
of the radiators, creaking rafters; or later when you begin
opening closets and drawers, searching my papers
for what to keep, what to throw away, what means
nothing; when you put your hand inside a pants pocket
and find my pocket knife and yourself breathless,
remember. When you walk Portland Avenue
to the ice pond at the end, watch me, hunched over
your skates, tightening the laces; visit the hours
memory enshrines, the hours of pitching baseballs
in the street, the afternoon lunches on Grand Avenue.
Gather the sunflowers or irises from the backyard,
and when you feel sad, thinking we were unfinished,
remember flowers feel no grief, the wind no guilt
for breaking branches. Remember the door between us
now swings on its hinges both ways; the moment
I close my eyes to you I open them to eternity,
just on the other side. Only a wink separates us.

Thomas R. Smith

Affectionate Witness

On my birthday
my father would phone
faithfully to recall
that subzero January
morning he drove
my mother to the hospital:
"We had a new
forty-seven Chevy.
It was fifty below, and
I could barely scrape a hole
to see out the windshield."

Listening, I'd envision
the Chevy cautiously
rounding the slippery
curves of the River Road
in darkness, the same
route Dad drove us
five years later,
the August my brother
Terry arrived,
the river metallic in sun-
light and my face
buried in a Blackhawk
comic all the way
to St. Joe's.

Each birthday I'd press
the receiver closer
to hear the old man's

burred recitation, and later
chuckle over the repetitions
of age without ever
admitting to myself
the renewal that came
with the simple ritual,
which now that he's gone
is one of those things
I miss most
about my father,
his affectionate witness
to three or four details
that made the story real,
and by which again
and again I was born.

Kathleen Patrick

COMMUTING

I think of you
When I am driving in my car,
On the way to work,
Picking up something at the grocery store,
Rushing for a quick workout.
There are other times, yes,
But the car is where you are closest.
You sit somewhere behind me, your voice
Not really there, but I can imagine it.
And when you laugh, I feel it
Through my chest and stomach;
You laugh more now.

You seem perplexed.
How could things have gotten so muddy?
Family slipped away,
Days rolled over to years,
Too many angry words
Said in haste.
But, mostly, I feel you smiling
When I recall the part of the past
That was worth photographing.
And when something has gone well
In my day, you seem to be there,
For the ride home,
Telling me how proud you are,
How you always knew I had it in me.

Mary Rose O'Reilley

TWIN

The incubator
was not lens enough
to show me where you flew,
out of the doctor's fingers,

out of the air's restraint.
And all their mirrors
could not lure your breath.
You were the part of me

that gave itself to death.
Sometimes I dream of eyes,
sealed with a membrane
of unknowing

like a mystic's veil,
that open to my glance
without surprise.
Sometimes I dream

of perfect understanding.
Sometimes I snatch
at hands that seem to seek
as through a caul.

Sometimes I waken
With an infant's shriek.

Margaret Hasse

BASKET, RIVER

A baby placed
in a well-woven basket
of adoption
moves with the flow
that carries its little life
from one woman
to another whose arms
are ready to tend,
whose body has remained empty
of what she is in need of carrying,
who plucks the bundle
from among the bulrushes,
out of the stream.

I stand at the river,
thinking of the woman
upstream, how in the middle
of hardship and loss,
she had faith
in a small basket, a big river,
that someone with strong arms
would pull her beloved son
from the current, lift him high,
raise him to manhood,
the child of two mothers
who labored in different ways
believing in water's unbroken stream.

*— for all women who have chosen
adoption for a child they bore*

Katrina Vandenberg

The Young Widow's Conception Of Faith

After he died, a stranger planted a tree for him,
an olive in the rock of Israel. When his widow
washed her dish and swept her porch, she thought
about him growing there, sap turned to blood.
Years later when she has grown still more
and been married again and blessed more times
than she can count, the tree will curl its leaves
upon the bluest sky and shed branches in peace.
Oil will be pressed and flow from his fruit, softening
a woman's skin, a crust of bread, lighting
a rag lamp after dark. His branches will be spoons,
whistles, umbrellas, and strangers everywhere
will smell his unbruised olive flesh and hold him,
loving the straightness of his olive bones.

Roberta Hill Whiteman

CURRENTS

How differently the river gleams
now you are gone.
Once it rushed headlong
down the plain,
polishing the canyon stone
until the fluted edges
filled with fire,
but now two currents churn,
converging in a single ripple
that never reaches shore.
Like a diamondback
migrating to mountains,
the ripple culls the current;
the far half jumps with light,
sending all shadow
back along the ridge,
while the other is subdued,
measuring an obscure song,
deep as plunder, doubly lost.

Some said you were unhappy,
that you had planned
to travel tomorrow.
Tomorrow. The right cadence,
the right words are wedged
in the hoof of the horse
that took you
beyond the clatter of dishes
and toys, beyond the market
bartering rifles,

beyond broken glass
or the need for shoes.
I believe your beloved
rode that dark stallion,
so much like the one
he owned before the war.
At last he came to carry you
over the dim shimmer of mountains,
along the white road
into the smoke of stars.

Worlds upon worlds
the stallion restored
you to your beloved.
We couldn't call you back,
lovely autumn mother
with a face so like the moon.
Please look once again,
for at last we're learning
to live as you have taught,
taking time to love each day,
to live without regret.
Now each of us must suffer
his own spirit,
and catch the starlight
aging in his hands.
Now each of us knows the river
will never be the same,
and sometimes it gets hard
to see the undiscovered depth,
or to hear the wind
singing above our cries.

In memory of Eva Whiteman

APARTMENTS OF THE DEAD

Somewhere along in your forties,
You realize a lot of people are dead,
But not you. Not yet.
Driving past the hospital, you recall
That curly-haired medical student
Her quick hands, her eager mouth.
She had a sweet apartment above the park,
Fragrant with eucalyptus. Remember
Those silly games you played
With her silver stethoscope? She lost
Both breasts, those breasts you used to kiss.
She's gone. And you can't believe you can't
Visit your pal, the poet,
Whose tiny apartment was jammed
With books, laundry, beer cans,
Ash trays big as hub caps.
You'd clear a space and smoke
And smoke and laugh and laugh.
That room smelled bad
But also good. He's gone,
Beneath the snow, beneath the earth.
You drive by your grandmother's place.
When she opened the door, she'd shout your name
And if she'd won the lottery, then add,
Immediately, "You want something to eat?"
She had stubble on her chin
And a glint in her eye
And she shared a juicy story
She'd been keeping warm for weeks.
She wore too much perfume,

But it couldn't cut the odor
Of coffee in that room.
Perhaps you don't miss these people
As much as you miss their apartments,
Those little chatterboxes,
Those friendly, small efficiencies.
You imagine two men making love
In that quiet place above the park,
An old woman stroking her cat
In the poet's rank apartment,
A retarded man struggling
To open a can of tuna in that room
Where your grandmother laughed
Over photographs of her youth.
How sad, you think. How strange.
Then the car behind you honks,
And you see that the light has changed.

Dobby Gibson

ENCROACHMENT

To those who say time
conquers all philosophy,
I wonder what you make of this
and the reasons long dreamed of,
but like our reflections,
always one step too late.
It is November again.
The leaves are falling,
and then, as if that weren't enough,
the rain is, too.
True to its mission,
the cold makes us feel old.
Over what we were
and never fully are.
What we saved, or hoped for,
what we found and whom we never will.
Rain on my skylight.
Rain by any other name.
And like any prayer
it seems to hold out hope,
like the books we always had our heads in
while still pretending otherwise,
swearing to our selves
that if we ever did find
a way out of this we'd never ask
for anything again,
content to be these prematurely old souls,
ordering out of habit,
unable to recall what any
should finally be remembered for:

their bread, or way with the truth,
or even this very air, like greater breathing,
right here, speaking of autumn nights
as if filled with a new voice
larger than our own.

Susan Steger Welsh

AFTER LEARNING COYOTE ARGUED AGAINST IMMORTALITY FOR HUMANS

The Turks say death is a black camel
that kneels at everyone's gate.
The English say death keeps no calendar.
The Jews say dying while young is a boon in old age.
When doctors say, *There's nothing else we can do,*
my friend asks me, *What do I do next? What do I do now?*
The French say there is no dying by proxy.
The board outside God's Church of Everlasting Joy says,
Signs Are Everywhere.
The plants scatter seeds.
The Chinese say people live like birds in a tree:
when the time comes, each takes flight.
The misprint in the prayer book says,
Life up your hearts to the Most High.
In the dream my soul says Owl. Fish.
The mathematicians say zero holds up everything.

Ray Gonzalez

LAST NIGHT

Last night I thought the Martians came.
Don't laugh.

It was only me, waking from a dream
where my father was dying,

spinning out of the heavens to ask forgiveness
for staying up there too long.

Last night, I was his son and he lifted me
in his arms before he hit the earth.

The explosion was amazing and I woke up
with a beard on my face.

Last night, I slept as if I was
the last man in the family,

an old, confused stranger trying
every locked door, unable to get in.

I kept sleeping when the man finally
entered through the broken window,

shards of glass in his hair
as blinding as the stars.

James Cihlar

LAST YEAR

What we do not know about fate
Harms us less than what we think we know.

We think we know the rate of exchange,
As if we can trade off years of estrangement

With deathbed forgiveness,
A life of sinning

With one true repentance,
But we cannot. Fate will catch up.

Fate does not tell time with clocks.
It does not enter with the creak of the stair

We hear from our bed alone
In a house wrapped in dark,

As we count the muffled footsteps in the hallway,
Measuring the shrinking distance from our pillow.

It will never come at a time
That allows us to anticipate arrival.

It would sooner show up the moment before
We bury our face in sleep

Exhaling the last worry of day.
Fate moves with the staccato bounce

Of an alley cat on winter ice.
It visits us as a car accident en route

To a job interview
The day after we were fired from the previous job –

Bestowing one blow
On the heels of another –

As if to say, you thought you had me figured out,
You thought you were safe.

G. E. Patterson

Letter from the Dead

One of the four rivers is gray like sky.
The gray of factory dust, of old men
sleeping on the old benches in the park.
The gray of your hair everywhere, I'd guess,
though I haven't seen you in a long time.

If you're bald, don't tell me. Keep your bad news
a secret. I want to remember
you as you were—but with gray in your hair,
a mark of wisdom and maturity
and the sorrow you've had to accept.

If your memory is good, you'll remember—
the single bed, its sheets grayed from washings;
the light almost as thin as it is
today; a black fan spreading the stale air.
I lay naked while you peeled oranges,
a sheet bunched in your lap; juice raining down
in a sunburst; thin and slightly sour
sections of fruit cradled in your left hand.
I ate each one you gave me—quickly, greedily,
without chewing. The way I still do, now
and again. Remembering happiness
is not an agony. It's still happiness.

Ann Iverson

In Every Minute of Every Hour of Every Day

All winter long and then some into early spring
    either the moon or the sun followed or led the way.

And in every minute when they divulge
    their round and serious request

between collected branch and cloud,
    I understand that I am needed

to sweep their petals of light that fall around my steps,
    to provide focus for them so far away,

to find words for a friend's life broken
    to clean time's closet where too much is stored of every hour.

And I try to consider how life works.
    And I try to consider how I fit in to this extraordinary plan.

And sometimes with a troubled mind
    (but not always) I find no resolution.

So in the mirror I apply bright red lips
    to this portrait of a woman considering and considering.

And sometimes I look over to the other side
    and see myself and know that in the sweet,

sad coming and going in every minute
    of every hour of every day, I have changed.

Morgan Grayce Willow

FURTHEST LIMIT

Silvered undersides
of oak leaves shiver
in the humid summer

wind that rides a wave
of heat up from the soybean
field across the highway.

The thick carpet of acorns
crunches under my sandals
as I pass beneath the oaks,

their dry cackle
like the voice of the dying.
Always, there is someone

taking that journey.
Last night I dreamt
you were the one

stepping out on that twisting
path, though it's been
more than a decade

since you said goodbye
in a raspy voice.
You led

the march in my dream,
though it soon became
a procession of all

my departed, each
crushed acorn another
voice of farewell.

One by one, I climb
metal stairs spiraling up
inside an old, brick

water tower, paper
and a good pen
tucked under my arm.

The voices pull
against my calves
like gravity.

From the circular room
at the top of the tower,
I look through the crowns

of oaks, the dark sides
of their leaves now shifting
with the roll of breeze

that presses on to the soybeans,
the whole field lifting
its mass of silver under-leaves.

My penance,
and my offering,
is to remember,

and to notice
the continual
farewell.

. . . and a bird sings

Joyce Sutphen

Now That Anything Could Happen

You now know that anything could happen;
things that never happened before, things that
only happened in movies and nightmares
are happening now, as if nothing could
stop them. You know now that you are not safe,
you know you live in fragile skin and bones,
that even steel and concrete can melt away,
and that the earth itself can come unhinged,
shaken from its orbit around the sun.
You know, now that anything can happen,
it's hard to know what will, and what will you
do now that you know? What words will you say
now that you could say anything? What hands
will you hold? Whose heart will beat inside you?

Greg Watson

Frank Sinatra Changing Limos
(circa 1991)

Lessons in impermanence are everywhere. Once,
when I was young, I saw Frank Sinatra after a
performance step into one limousine, hunker down,
and enter another. It was so seamless, so practiced,
that no one seemed to notice. This is how death
must be I think. Others will be saddened, searching
for us, confused, pounding their hands on the
window of an empty car. Meanwhile we'll be
drinking Chivas Regal, talking to the president long
distance, slowly pulling out into the dark and
boundless night.

Jorie Miller

Dust

for Glenn Hokenson 1954-1989

I spent the months after you died
walking with my daughter.
All summer I pulled stones out of her mouth,
all summer heavy machinery
dragged past our house.
Dust lifted off the raw road,
clouded the air and fell again.
It was dry,
so dry nothing held the fine earth in place.
Somehow your death made me calm
as real things can do.
Not the same as waking in the night
fearing a plane dropping onto the house
or a maniac killing your child.
Words, they don't stop the dying –
say street, Rose, say knee, say flower.
Life has gone on, dear friend –
a summer past, a new season rises.
There is so much life, we can never keep it down.

John Reinhard

Where To Find Heaven

If you're a gnat
you move simply
to the underside
of your mate's wing
where the shelter
and the updrafts
seem exceptional,
where you might flutter
at the entrance
to the cavern of
a cow's ear, flutter
until even the cow
begins to imagine the air
more musical than
the usual stutter
through tall grass.

Some time ago
my grandmother
from her sickbed
told the nurse to call
the priest. To call family close.
When the priest came,
she folded her hands
in final prayer, and died,
the air still as dust in places
where wind hides.
For my grandmother, heaven
was the rediscovery
of her lover's wide shoulders
as well as the new

voices of all the lost,
every root traced, at last.
Here, William Butler Yeats
could sing her lullabyes
for one sleep
that would never come.

Pascal once said
that a belief
in Heaven is a kind of Heaven
all its own.
He said this in French,
a language
I doubt. I doubt
the whiteness of frost.
The quickening
of our days. I doubt
that we are much beyond
our inclinations
toward more
solid ground.

But I like the notion
that Yeats sings us all
to a sleep
of waking. I like as well
the possibility
that a thing light
as a gnat
might know the fullness
of this life. And that I
might fly somehow
beyond this flesh I am
and love
to be of heart and wing
the constant
fluttering.

Susan Marie Swanson

Trouble, Fly

Trouble, fly
out of our house.
We left the window
open for you.

Fly like smoke from a chimney.
Fly like the whistle from a train.
Fly far, far
away from my family,
mumbling in their sleep.

Trouble, fly.
Let our night
be a night of peace.

Louis Jenkins

Yellow Hat

Nobody knows what will happen, what catastrophes, what miraculous transformations. In order to maintain faith, to plan for the future, the world must be simplified. Here is the window out of which you can see a tree, a bright red flower, green grass extending over the hill. There is a tree with an orange bird, and on the very top of the hill, yes, there I am…two legs, two arms, ten fingers like sausages and a smile on my big round face. And just six inches above my yellow hat the blue sky begins.

Jude Nutter

CROWS

I saw that strange blend of softness
and brittle energy in the shattered wing,

and the blue that floated beneath the surface
of its feathers – sometimes the flesh is a mirror

but it's never this world that's reflected.
There was nothing on the beach of interest

except this body. As I moved away
they came down, out of the trees – after the first,

an avalanche – to stand fussing
in a circle around their dead companion.

They were there until the tide came in,
lifted that broken body up on its hem, turned,

and floated it out – an untidy blackness riding
into view, then vanishing, with each swell.

All they did was wait there. Keeping vigil.
That's all. There are times when this world

Is just enough like paradise.

Margaret Hasse

MEADOWLARK: MENDING SONG

What hurt you today
was taken out of your heart
by the meadowlark
who slipped the silver needle
of her song
in and out of the grey day
and mended what was torn.

Jere Truer

THE WHOLE CATASTROPHE

It has been nine years in this house,
thirteen in this neighborhood.
The waitress at the local café
asks me if I'll have the usual.
I never thought I'd be predictable.
And yet I've come to covet the reliable,
the time worn, the perennial ways
that men and women have on this earth.

We spend today raking leaves,
caulking the cracks, keeping winter
and all its rodential companions outside.
I'll take this seasonal death of crumbling
rock, fallen leaves, and soft ground.
I'll call it life. I'll call it home.
On this I rely for the time we have
Together – this whole catastrophe of love.

Wang Ping

from GREAT SUMMONS

> *A ritual song from 300 B.C., China, to call the souls of the dead to return home*

All stories are personal.

must be told,
and retold till they blossom
between our lips, take roots
in the belly buttons, till the currents
of sap, thicker than blood,
roar in our veins, till eyes
can open again to the blazing sun,
and the moon no longer weeps in the dreams
of children, till every name, face,
every shattered hope, calls
from the womb of memory:

> *"Let some goodness*
> *come out of our deaths.*
> *Let the pain of the living*
> *bear some fruit."*

Acknowledgments

We wish to express our thanks to authors, publishers and other copyright holders for permission to include the works below. Every effort has been made to identify copyright holders and obtain permission.

Patricia Barone, excerpts from "The Life Is Greater Than the Body" from *Handmade Paper*. Copyright 1994 by Patricia Barone. Reprinted with the permission of New Rivers Press, www.newriverspress.com.

Marilyn Benson, "Good-bye." Used with the permission of the author.

John Berryman, Dream Songs #172 "Your face broods from my table" and #207 "—How are you?" from *The Dream Songs*. Copyright 1969 by John Berryman. Copyright renewed by Kate Donahue Berryman. Reprinted with permission of Farrar, Straus and Giroux, LLC.

Carol Pearce Bjorlie, "Ambushed" from *Window*. A chapbook. Used with the permission of the author.

Robert Bly, "Looking at Aging Faces," from *Morning Poems*. New York: HarperCollins, 1997. Used with the permission of the author.

Robert Bly, "Snowbanks North of the House," from *Eating the Honey of Words: New and Selected Poems*. New York: HarperCollins, 1999. Used with the permission of the author.

Marilyn J. Boe, "A Strange Thing Happens," in *Sidewalks* #8. Spring/Summer 1995. Used with the permission of the author.

Todd Boss, "Don't Come Home" from *Yellowrocket*. New York: W.W. Norton & Company, 2008. Used with the permission of the author.

Ted Bowman, "Male Tears" and "Soften the Blow." Earlier versions were published in the *Journal of Pastoral Care*, Spring 1990 and in *Crossroads: Stories at the Intersections*. Bethlehem: Moravian Church Publications, 2008. Used with permission of the author.

Jill Breckenridge, "Drawing of My Family: Age 6" from *How To Be Lucky*. Emporia State University: Bluestem Books, 1990. Used with the permission of the author.

Breitenbucher, Annie. "Silver Spoons on Glass" and "Worth" from *Fortune*. St. Paul: Laurel Poetry Collective, 2006. Used with the permission of the author.

Betty Bridgman, "Companioned" from *This Is Minnesota*. St Paul: North Central Publishing Company, 1958. Copyright by Betty Bridgman. Reprinted with the permission of George H. Bridgman for the Estate of Betty Bridgman.

Lucille Broderson, "Eight of Us" and "Wild Geese" from *A Thousand Years*. Johnstown, OH: Pudding House Press, 2002. Used with the permission of the author.

Lucille Broderson, "In the End" from *Beware: Poems*. Minneapolis: Spout Press, 2002. Used with the permission of the author.

Michael Dennis Browne, "Dream at the Death of James Wright" and "Neighbor in May" from *Smoke From The Fires*. Pittsburgh: Carnegie-Mellon University Press, 1985. Used with the permission of the author.

Philip Bryant, "First Christmas After the Divorce" from *Sermon on a Perfect Spring Day*. Copyright 1998 by Philip Bryant. Reprinted with the permission of New Rivers Press, www.newriverspress.com.

John Caddy, "Touching" from *The Color of Mesabi Bones: Poems and Prose Poems*. Minneapolis: Milkweed Editions, 1989. Used with the permission of the author.

Sharon Chmielarz, "After the Dance" from *But I Won't Go Out in a Boat*. Copyright 1991 by Sharon Chmielarz. Reprinted with the permission of New Rivers Press, www.newriverspress.com.

Sharon Chmielarz, "Joe" from *Different Arrangements*. Copyright 1982 by Sharon Chmielarz. Reprinted with the permission of New Rivers Press, www.newriverspress.com.

James Cihlar, "Last Year" from *Undoing*. Seekonk, MA: Little Pear Press, 2008. Used with the permission of the author.

Carol Connolly, "Divorced" from *Payments Due*. St. Paul: Midwest Villages and Voices, 1985. Used with the permission of the author.

Florence Chard Dacey, "Widows" from *The Swoon*. Brewster, MN: The Kraken Press, 1979. Used with the permission of the author.

Kirsten Dierking, "For the Disappeared" from *Northern Oracle*. Minneapolis: Spout Press, 2007. Used with the permission of the author.

Kirsten Dierking, "The Pleasure of Safety" from *One Red Eye: Poems*. Duluth: Holy Cow! Press, 2001. Used with the permission of the author.

Norita Dittberner-Jax, "Crossing" from *The Watch*. St. Paul: Whistling Shade Press, 2008. Used with the permission of the author.

John Engman, "Think of Me in D Major" from *Temporary Help: Poems*. Copyright 1998 by John Engman. Reprinted with the permission of Holy Cow! Press, www.holycowpress.org.

Heid Erdrich, "Phosphorescence" and "The Widow's Grove" from *Fishing for Myth*. Copyright 1997 by Heid Erdrich. Reprinted with the permission of New Rivers Press, www.newriverspress.com.

Ann Iverson, "When a Son Goes Off to War" from *Definite Space: Poems*. Duluth: Holy Cow! Press, 2007. Used with permission of the author.

Ann Iverson, "In Every Minute of Every Hour of Every Day." Used with the permission of the author.

Louis Jenkins, "Yellow Hat." Used with the permission of the author.

Elizabeth Bourque Johnson, "From Room to Room," in *Sing Heavenly Muse!* 1986. Used with the permission of the author.

Elizabeth Bourque Johnson, "The Woman Who Wailed" in *Journey Notes*. Ed. Richard Solly and Roseann Lloyd. San Francisco: Harper and Row, 1989. Used with the permission of the author.

Jean McKenzie Johnson, "Echoes." Used with permission of the author.

Deborah Keenan, "Blue Heron" from *Willow Room, Green Door*. Minneapolis: Milkweed Editions, 2007. Used with permission of the author.

Deborah Keenan, "Comfort" from *Happiness*. Minneapolis: Coffee House Press, 1995. Used with the permission of the author.

Stanley Kiesel, "Doris" in *25 Minnesota Poets*. Ed. Seymour Yesner. Minneapolis: Nodin Press, 1974. Used with the permission of the author.

Susan Deborah King, "Twinges" from *One-Breasted Woman: Poems*. Duluth: Holy Cow! Press, 2007. Used with the permission of the author.

Patricia Kirkpatrick, "The Black Squirrel." *Century's Road*. Duluth, MN: Holy Cow! Press, 2004. Used with the permission of the author.

Evelyn Klein, "Tornado Country" from *From Here Across the Bridge*. Minneapolis: Nodin Press, 2006. Used with the permission of the author.

Kathryn Kysar, "Another Postcard from Chinook" from *Dark Lake*. Bemidji, MN: Loonfeather Press, 2002. Used with the permission of the author.

Ed-Bok Lee, "At Mihwangsa Temple" from *Real Karaoke People*. Copyright 2005 by Ed-Bok Lee. Reprinted with the permission of New Rivers Press, www.newriverspress.com.

Alex Lemon, "Ashtray" from *Mosquito*. Portland, OR: Tin House Books, 2006. Reprinted with the permission of Tin House Books.

James Lenfestey, "Driving Across Wisconsin" from *Saying Grace*. Marshfield, WI: Marsh River Editions, 2004. Used with the permission of the author.

Meridel LeSueur, "Dead in Bloody Snow" from *Rites of Ancient Ripenings*. Minneapolis: Vanilla Press, 1975. Used with the permission of Jocelyn Tilsen for the Estate of Meridel LeSueur.

Roseann Lloyd, "this child" from *Tap Dancing for Big Mom*. St. Paul: New Rivers Press, 1986. Used with the permission of the author.

Mary Logue, "Blue" from *Meticulous Attachment: Poems*. Minneapolis: Mid-List Press, 2005. Used with the permission of the author.

E'ireann Lorsung, "Poem for Your Brother" forthcoming in *Projet Linguistique*, Milkweed Editions, 2011. Used with the permission of the author.

Freya Manfred, "Three Christmases Ago" from *A Goldenrod Will Grow*. Minneapolis: James D. Thueson, 1971. Used with the permission of the author.

Caroline Vogel Marshall, "I Dream the Divorce Is Final" in *25 Minnesota Poets*. Ed. Seymour Yesner. Minneapolis: Nodin Press, 1974. Used with the permission of the author.

Eugene McCarthy, "Courage at Sixty" from *Selected Poems*. Red Wing, MN: Lone Oak Press, 1997. Reprinted with the permission of Lone Oak Press, An Imprint of Finney Company.

Thomas McGrath, "News of Your Death" from *Echoes Inside the Labyrinth*. New York: Thunder's Mouth Press, 1983, p. 88.

Thomas McGrath, "Remembering Loves and Deaths" from *Selected Poems: 1938-1988*. Copyright 1988 by Thomas McGrath. Reprinted with the permission of Copper Canyon Press, www.coppercanyonpress.org.

Linda Back McKay, "The Art of Grieving" from *The Cockeyed Precision Of Time: New And Selected Poems*. Minneapolis: White Space Press, 2007. Used with the permission of the author.

Ethna McKiernan, "Elegy Against the Dying of the Light" from *Caravan*. Minneapolis: Midwest Villages and Voices, 1989. Used with the permission of the author.

Ethna McKiernan, "Grief" from *The One Who Swears You Can't Start Over*. Clare, Ireland: Salmon Publishing Ltd. 2002. Used with the permission of the author.

Bill Meissner, "The Dance of the Ripples" from *American Compass*. Notre Dame, IN: University of Notre Dame Press, 2004. Used with the permission of the author.

Jorie Miller, "Dust" in *ArtWord Quarterly*. Fall 1996. Used with the permission of the author.

Leslie Adrienne Miller, "Sundays When Their Laps Were full of Light" from *Eat Quite Everything You See: Poems*. St. Paul: Graywolf Press, 2002. Used with the permission of the author.

John Minczeski, "Grandfather Janosz and the Polish Graves of New Prague" from *Gravity*. Lubbock, TX: Texas Tech University Press, 1991. Used with the permission of the author.

Jim Moore, "It Is Not the Fact That I Will Die That I Mind" and "Seven Invisible Strings" from *Lightning At Dinner: Poems.* St. Paul: Graywolf Press, 2005. Used with the permission of the author.

David Mura, "Hope Without Hope" from *After We Lost Our Way*. New York: E.P. Dutton, 1989. Used with the permission of the author.

Tim Nolan, "For My Country in Its Darkness" from *The Sound of It.* Moorhead, MN: New Rivers Press, 2008. Used with the permission of the author.

Jude Nutter, "Crows" and excerpt from "Meditations: Tyne Cot Cemetery, Ypres" from *The Curator of Silence.* Notre Dame, IN: The University of Notre Dame Press, 2007. Used with the permission of the author.

Monica Ochtrup, "Lost" from *Pieces from the Long Afternoon.* Copyright 1991 by Monica Ochtrup. Reprinted with the permission of New Rivers Press, www.newriverspress.com.

Mary Rose O'Reilley, "Twin" from *Half Wild: Poems.* Copyright 2006 by Mary Rose O'Reilley. Reprinted with the permission of Louisiana State University Press.

Joe Paddock, "Earth Tongues" from *Earth Tongues.* Minneapolis: Milkweed Publications, 1985. Used with the permission of the author.

Nancy Paddock, "Asleep in Jesus" from *A Dark Light.* Minneapolis: Vanilla Press, 1978. Used with the permission of the author.

Kathleen Patrick, "Commuting." Used with permission of the author.

G. E. Patterson, "Letter from the Dead" from *Tug.* Copyright 1999 by G. E. Patterson. Reprinted with the permission of Graywolf Press, Minneapolis, MN, www.graywolfpress.org.

Wang Ping, excerpt from "The Great Summons" and "Tsunami Chant" from *The Magic Whip.* St. Paul: Coffee House Press, 2003. Used with the permission of the author.

Spencer Reece, excerpt from "Addresses" and "Interlude" from *The Clerk's Tale.* Copyright 2004 by Spencer Reese. Reprinted with the permission of Houghton Mifflin Harcourt Publishing Company.

William Reichard, "In Florida" from *This Brightness.* Minneapolis: Mid-List Press, 2007. Used with the permission of the author.

John Reinhard, "Where to Find Heaven" from *On the Road to Patsy Cline.* Copyright 1996 by John Reinhard. Reprinted with the permission of New Rivers Press, www.newriverspress.com.

John Calvin Rezmerski, "Elegy for Spectators" and "Second Marriage" from *What Do I Know?* Duluth, MN: Holy Cow! Press, 2000. Used with the permission of the author.

Gail Rixen, "His Mother" from *Pictures of 3 Seasons*. Copyright 1991 by Gail Rixen. Reprinted with the permission of New Rivers Press, www.newriverspress.com.

George Roberts, "lament" from *Scrut*. Minneapolis: Holy Cow! Press, 1983. Used with the permission of the author.

Beverly Rollwagen, "Sharing" from *Flying: prose / poems*. Minneapolis: Nodin Press, 2009. Used with the permission of the author.

Ruth Roston, "Players" in *25 Minnesota Poets #2*. Ed. Seymour Yesner. Minneapolis: Nodin Press, 1977. Used with the permission of Nodin Press.

Mary Kay Rummel, "Camouflage" and "Symbiosis" from *Green Journey, Red Bird*. Bemidji, MN: Loonfeather Press, 2001. Used with the permission of the author.

Larry Schug, "Windstorm" in *The Cancer Poetry Project*. Ed. Karin B. Miller. Minneapolis: Fairview Press, 2001. Used with the permission of the author.

Su Smallen, "Crenellation" from *Weight of Light*. St. Paul: Laurel Poetry Collective, 2004. Used with the permission of the author.

Thomas R. Smith, "Affectionate Witness" from *The Dark Indigo Current*. Duluth: Holy Cow! Press, 2000. Used with the permission of the author.

Anna Irena Sochocky, "Time Between Hours." Used with permission of the author.

Richard Solly, "One Morning Cereal" and "When I Die." Used with permission of the author.

Madelon Sprengnether, excerpt from "Anniversary" from *The Angel of Duluth*. Buffalo: White Pine Press, 2006. Used with the permission of the author.

Joyce Sutphen, "Now That Anything Can Happen" from *Naming the Stars*. Copyright 2004 by Joyce Sutphen. Reprinted with the permission of Holy Cow! Press, www.holycowpress.org.

Barton Sutter, "Apartments of the Dead" from *Farewell to the Starlight in Whiskey*. Copyright 2004 by Barton Sutter. Reprined with the permission of BOA Editions, Ltd., www.boaeditions.org.

Susan Marie Swanson, "Trouble, Fly." Copyright 1997 by Susan Marie Swanson. Used with the permission of the author.

Jere Truer, "The Whole Catastrophe" in *Speakeasy* (January-February 2003) volume 1, number 3. Used with the permission of the author.

Warren Woessner, "The Disappearance of My Father" from *Storm Lines*. St. Paul: New Rivers Press, 1987. Used with the permission of the author.

David Wojahn, Part VII of the poem sequence "The Shades" from *The Falling Hour*. Copyright 1997. Reprinted with the permission of the University of Pittsburgh Press www.upress.pitt.edu.

James Wright, "Three Steps to the Graveyard" from *The Branch Will Not Break*. Copyright 1963 by James Wright. Reprinted with the permission of Wesleyan University Press www.wesleyan.edu/wespress.

Pam Wynn, "Epilepsy: This Is What I Know" and "Miscarriage" from *Diamonds on the Back of a Snake*. St. Paul: Laurel Poetry Collective, 2004. Used with the permission of the author.

Nolan Zavoral, "Young Blond Guy at Piano." Used with the permission of the author.

Index of Poets

ELIZABETH BOURQUE JOHNSON, Ph.D. encountered grief first as a nurse and nurse-educator. When personal grief confronted her at the death of her daughter, she began to write poetry. Classes at the Loft came next, followed by an MA in Creative Writing and a PhD in literature at the University of Minnesota, where she has taught both writing and literature. She developed a course called "Writing through Grief," offered through the Loft and the University's Compleat Scholar Program. She speaks to grief groups throughout the Twin Cities, including the Sudden Infant Death Foundation and Compassionate Friends.

Elizabeth has also written and edited in the health field, including about medical ethics. Her poetry has won local and nationwide awards and has appeared in the literary press in the US and Canada.

She can be contacted at johns268@umn.edu

TED BOWMAN is an author and educator whose work includes a specialty in change and transition and the resulting grief and loss. He uses poetry, memoir, writing, and other literary tools to aid people in re-storying their lives. Ted has also taught Family Education courses at the University of Minnesota since 1981. He served on the board of the National Association for Poetry Therapy from 1999 to 2008. Ted is the author of over 80 articles and chapters appearing in a range of books, journals, newspapers, and magazines. His booklet, *Loss of Dreams: A Special Kind of Grief*, was released in 1994. *Finding Hope When Dreams Have Shattered* was published in 2001. *Crossroads: Stories at the Intersections*, a book of poems and essays, was released in 2008.

He can be contacted at bowma008@umn.edu

Made in the USA
Lexington, KY
17 November 2019